To Jerry,

who champions

my dreams

Acknowledgments

This dream of a book wouldn't be possible without the many people I have known who have dared to dream big dreams and courageously realize them. My deepest thanks to all the participants in *Creating a Culture of Renewal*® (and predecessor iterations) who have contributed so much to refine the process of renewal, and who have demonstrated through their ministries that this process really works. Special thanks to members of my teaching faculty, past and present, including Doug Wasinger, Margaret Gillikin, Les Huseby, Mary Beth Taylor, Ralph Lepley, Martha Taylor, Steve Trout, McKenzie Sefa, Bonnie Marden, and Adrianne Coleman, whose alignment and belief I treasure.

To my amazing team at Rebekah Simon-Peter Coaching and Consulting Inc., including Ann Miller and Nikki Kranzler-Gacke who make sure I am always where I am supposed to be and that I have everything thing I need when I get there. To Laura Bush, the Writers in Residence, and the Wisdom Writers Guild who coaxed this book into the light of day. Grateful thanks to Donna Annis, Sam, Abraham, Louise, and the Landmark community for teaching me the secrets of transformation.

Unending thanks to my husband, Jerry, for not lifting his eyebrows in alarm every time I propose yet another dream. Lastly, to Jesus who dared to dream the biggest dream of all.

Other books by Rebekah Simon-Peter

Green Church: Reduce, Reuse, Recycle, Rejoice!

Green Church: Reduce, Reuse, Recycle, Rejoice! Leader Guide
with Pamela Dilmore

7 Simple Steps to Green Your Church

The Jew Named Jesus:
Discover the Man and His Message

DREAM
like
JESUS®

Deepen Your Faith and
Bring the Impossible to Life

BY REBEKAH SIMON-PETER

Foreword by Mike Slaughter

DREAM LIKE JESUS®
Deepen Your Faith and Bring the Impossible to Life

Author: Rebekah Simon-Peter

Foreword by Mike Slaughter

©2019 Rebekah Simon-Peter

books@marketsquarebooks.com
P.O. Box 23664 Knoxville, Tennessee 37933

ISBN: 978-1-950899-04-3
Library of Congress: 2019943845

Printed and Bound in the United States of America
Cover Illustration & Book Design ©2019 Market Square Publishing, LLC
Publisher: Kevin Slimp
Editor: Kristin Lighter
Post-Process Editor: Ken Rochelle

Where noted, Scripture quotations are from:

(NRSV)
The New Revised Standard Version Bible, copyright © 1989 National
Council of the Churches of Christ in the United States of America.
Used by permission. All rights reserved worldwide.

(NIV)
THE HOLY BIBLE, NEW INTERNATIONAL VERSION®, NIV®
Copyright © 1973, 1978, 1984, 2011 by Biblica, Inc.® Used by permission.
All rights reserved worldwide.

(MSG)
Scripture quotations marked "MSG" or "The Message"
are taken from The Message. © 1993, 1994, 1995, 1996, 2000, 2001, 2002.
Used by permission of NavPress Publishing Group.

(ESV)
Scripture quotations are from The ESV® Bible (The Holy Bible, English
Standard Version®), copyright © 2001 by Crossway, a publishing ministry of
Good News Publishers. Used by permission. All rights reserved.

(NLT)
Scripture quotations marked (NLT) are taken from the Holy Bible, New Living Transla-
tion, copyright ©1996, 2004, 2015 by Tyndale House Foundation. Used by permission of
Tyndale House Publishers, Inc., Carol Stream, Illinois 60188. All rights reserved.

Table of Contents

Part Four: REALIZE the Dream

Part Five: EXPAND the Dream

Part Six: The Future is Yours

Foreword

The Bible has multiple accounts of ordinary people detecting the direction and voice of God through visions and dreams. The prophet Daniel could understand "visions and dreams of all kinds" (Dan. 1:17). God is revealed to the Old Testament prophets through visions and dreams. "Listen to my words: 'When there is a prophet among you, I, the Lord, reveal myself to them in visions, I speak to them in dreams'" (Numbers 12:6, NIV). The prophet Joel spoke of a future time when God would pour out the gift of God's Spirit on all people: "And afterward, I will pour out my Spirit on all people. Your sons and daughters will prophesy, your old men will dream dreams, your young men will see visions" (Joel 2:28).

Jesus appeared to the disciples multiple times after the resurrection, speaking often about his vision for the Kingdom of God. "Do not leave Jerusalem, but wait for the gift my Father promised, which you have heard me speak about. For John baptized with water, but in a few days you will be baptized with the Holy Spirit" (Acts 1:4-5). Ten days later on the day of Pentecost, Joel's ancient prophecy had been fulfilled (Acts 2:16-21).

The Apostle Peter, following Pentecost, becomes the norm for the Spirit-filled life. We can read about the account in the tenth chapter of Acts. The gentile centurion, Cornelius, has a vision of a messenger from God to send for Peter who was in the city of Joppa. This becomes a revolutionary point of universal inclusion for all of God's children.

Peter, in a concentrated time of prayer, "fell into a trance. He saw heaven opened and something like a large sheet being let down to earth" (Acts 10:11). The sheet contained all kinds of forbidden animals, birds, and reptiles according to Jewish dietary law. "Then a voice told him, 'Get up, Peter. Kill and eat'" (Acts 10:13). As an observant Jew, Peter refused at first. But the Spirit of God prevailed and Peter dared to dream Jesus' dream of the presence of God's new Kingdom order (Acts 11).

God didn't create us to sit around waiting to die so we can leave planet Earth and go to heaven. God created in each of us a unique God-dream for getting more heaven into planet Earth. We need to, in Rebekah Simon-Peter's words, "Dream like Jesus."

I am so blessed that I have been given a God-dream worth living and dying for. Without a God-dream, it becomes too easy to plateau and waste this precious gift of life. I have known too many people who hit their forties, fifties, and sixties, and just stop. Life for them begins to be about looking back instead of dreaming forward. Rebekah's book is a fresh reminder of the dream and possibilities that God has placed in each one of us. My prayer for you is that you dare to dream like Jesus!

Mike Slaughter
Pastor emeritus and global church ambassador for Ginghamsburg Church

PREFACE
Celebrate Everything

I was eight years old when I was confronted with my first kneeler. It was a jarring experience. Kneelers weren't standard furniture in the Reform Jewish Temple my family belonged to. But they were unavoidable in the Catholic church my best friend Diane and her family attended. As I watched the people around me kneel, I remembered having learned that Jews didn't bow down before any other gods but the one God, our God, of course. It was blasphemy.

There I was with Diane, her sister, and her parents. To kneel or not to kneel, that was my conundrum. I struck a compromise. I would sit on the edge of the hard, wooden pew, balancing carefully on my backside without actually sliding down far enough for my knees to touch the offending cushioned wood. I figured God would be okay with that.

Striking religious compromise was a skill I quickly acquired growing up with my Jewish mother, Catholic father, three brothers, and a sister. At our house, we did it all. We opened the front door for Elijah at Passover and for the Easter Bunny on Easter. Our living room sported a Christmas tree at Christmas and a Menorah at Chanukah. I grew up with a distinctly Jewish religious upbringing in a home where we celebrated everything.

We didn't, however, mention Jesus. My Dad had left the church and God of his youth by the time he married my mother on his twenty-first birthday. As for Jews, the word Jesus was verboten, his presence barely recognized.

So, while church was jarring for me, my experiences at Temple were uplifting. Temple gave me the outlines of God, and my rightful place in a community. I went to Shabbat services on Friday night, Sunday school on Sunday mornings – and as I approached the age of Bat Mitzvah – Hebrew School on Wednesday afternoons. I chanted my Torah portion in Hebrew at thirteen. At sixteen, I flew with my eight fellow confirmands and our rabbi on a class trip to Israel. I loved the sheer number of Jewish holidays, the heft of the Torah, the sacred music, the inspiring stories, the weight of tradition, the humor. And of course, the food. Especially the food.

Sex, Drugs, and Rock 'n Roll. But first, food.

There was a fair amount of conflict in my home growing up. I was on a quest for safety, for belonging. It took me deep into the comforts of excess food, then later the social ease of alcohol, and finally the otherworldly release of drugs. My weight fluctuated through my teens and twenties. At five feet three and one-quarter inches, ten extra pounds were noticeable. The more I managed and controlled what I ate, the worse it got.

Like a lot of girls, I dieted constantly. Even so, all I could think about was food, especially the kind that included flour and sugar. Later, I added other "coping skills" to my reper-toire: drinking and drugging. In practical terms, it meant that I had three problems on my hands – food, alcohol, and drugs – instead of one. After the trip to Israel at sixteen, I mostly stopped going to Temple. Like a lot of kids who are raised in church, I had all but graduated.

God, Again

My Jewish grandmother Miriam gifted me with a college graduation trip to Israel when I was twenty-two. We stayed with my Orthodox Jewish family in Jerusalem. Four weeks in the intensely Jewish environment of their home had re-awakened in me my love of Judaism and the presence of God. It also engendered a sense of belonging – to God, to community, and to a larger place in history.

Once I got back to the States, I began to participate in the Orthodox Jewish community. There were a few glitches in this new lifestyle. I had to dust off my skill of religious compromise to put my feminism on hold. In this traditional Jewish world, men and women had distinct gender roles including separate seating in *shul*. But it was worth it. I loved the sense of safety, the belonging, and the deep, rich learning and spirituality the community offered. My new rabbi was one very cool dude, even in his Chasidic garb and long side-curls. When he spoke, he radiated an authenticity and honesty that I had never before heard from a member of the clergy.

Recovery

Even with this wonderful sense of belonging, I still struggled with my weight. I was still getting high and still drinking to excess. One day, in my late twenties, engaged to be married to a *baal teshuva* (a newly Orthodox person like myself), the rabbi invited the two of us to join him in a spiritual approach found in a variety of addiction recovery circles.

The first meeting I went to included only Jews. But as cool as my rabbi was, I didn't really want to reveal my deepest secrets in front of him, or my fiancé, Doug. I found a different group to attend.

As it turns out, this new group wasn't like synagogue. And thankfully, even though it was held in a church, it wasn't like church either. People sat on couches that faced into the center of a room. There didn't seem to be an official leader. But this was clearly a community of people comfortable divulging their struggles with food. They revealed secrets I would never say out loud. There was a lot of openness and acceptance in the room, and a lot of love. I found it very meaningful, though odd. It was a different experience to talk openly about what I had hidden for years.

Many women and men spoke of a power greater than them-selves, a Higher Power at work in their lives. Some of the other women named Jesus as their Higher Power, others named God. The rest didn't elaborate. I had the sense that not everyone had the same concept of God, but that seemed to be okay.

This was the first time I had heard non-Jews talking about something as intimate as their experiences with God. Regardless of their religion, a mysterious, miraculous force for good was at work in their lives.

The whole thing was a mystery to me. Sure, I knew God. I respected God. But love? Not so much. Frankly, I wasn't sure God liked me. I felt I had to please God, to somehow keep him happy or at least stay off his bad side. But that was as far as our relationship went. I assumed God didn't want to get involved in any of the daily-ness of what I ate or didn't eat, or to give me any help in making the right choices.

So, I didn't ask.

That's not how the women and men around me talked about their experiences. "This morning when I woke up, I surrendered my life and my food to God. I asked God to help me make the right food choices today, to guide and direct me. And it worked! I haven't had to overeat all day."

Their God was supremely interested in the details of their lives and could be counted on for help in all manner of things. The more I went back to the room with couches to listen and, eventually, to talk, the more my life began to shift. I realized that when I, too, admitted aloud that I had a problem, and that I was powerless over that problem, I experienced a new sense of calm. They called this process "surrender." The more I practiced surrendering my life as it was, the more comfortable I became in my own skin.

Spirituality 101

Something else unusual was going on in these rooms. They called it "spirituality." They distinguished spirituality from religion. In fact, even though they talked about God, religion seemed to play little or no role. Each person was invited to relate to God in the way that made the most sense to them.

I liked this principle of permissiveness. Undefined by doctrine or creed, this spirituality was based in common principles found in major religious traditions, yet limited by none.

Instead of focusing on inherited understandings of God, or set beliefs about God, this principle of permissiveness restored to each person the freedom to directly experience God. It was also understood that no one person's understanding of God canceled out anyone else's. They trusted that more of God would be revealed to each person over time. There was no evangelizing, correcting, or coercing.

As I relaxed into this way of looking at things, I too followed their lead. I reached out to a power greater than myself for help with food, alcohol, and drugs. As my mind shifted from seeing my life as a fixed reality (this is just the way life is), to exploring new possibilities, (I could live free of the constant battle with food), sugar and caffeine came off the menu, without dieting.

The following year, alcohol and drugs also came off the menu. Flour took a while longer, but eventually, it came off too, again, without dieting. The desire to overeat, or to use drugs, or to drink was simply removed. In its place came a new self-confidence, trust in life, and freedom to be myself.

Seeing Jesus

On my twenty-eighth birthday, about a year into attending these meetings, I was squeaky clean, abstinent, and sober. That day I was in a re-birthing session with a trained facilitator named Stephanie. A thirty- or forty-something-year-old woman, she was caring and earnest. I was sure Stephanie held all the answers in her hands for me. As she led me through a guided meditation, I lay in a comfortable position in her office. My eyes were closed as I moved back in time.

Into this quiet, introspective space stepped an uninvited Jesus. When I least expected it, Jesus responded to my lifelong spiritual quest in a way I could never have predicted.

As Stephanie counted back the years, there Jesus stood before me. He was close enough for me to see the warmth in his eyes and the friendly creases around them. Even though I was awake, there was a dream-like quality to the whole experience. First, I knew who Jesus was, even though he resembled no picture I had ever seen, instead he was very Jewish looking. Second, he communicated without words, as happens in dreams sometimes. I knew what his gaze meant, even though he uttered no words. This very Jewish Jesus stood before me, radiating a knowing compassion. "I understand you," his eyes communicated. "All the decisions you've made and why you've wound up where you are. I love you. And I accept you, just as you are."

Jesus was speaking to me as though we had a relationship. This sense of connection surprised me, caught me off guard. I hadn't wanted or sought a relationship with him. Historically, the church had done terrible things to Jews in the name of Jesus. From the Crusades to Hitler – it all ran together for me. I was uncomfortable having Jesus in my world. Where was this connection with Jesus coming from?

By now, Stephanie had counted all the way back to the year of my birth. After a respectful pause, she checked in with me.

8

"Is there anything going on?" she inquired.

I never did tell Stephanie, but as soon as I burst through the door of the home I shared with Doug, I got on the phone with Teresa, my mentor from the recovery circle. She was a Christian who had recently enrolled in seminary. I figured she could shed some light on the whole experience.

I couldn't let this experience with Jesus alone. As I spoke more with Teresa about it, and others in my recovery circles, I realized I had experienced something fairly unusual. It wasn't until years later that it occurred to me that I had what people call "a born-again" experience in a re-birthing session.

That vision of Jesus lasted no more than thirty seconds, but it has been with me nearly thirty years. Even now, I get emotional thinking about it. It still floors me that he came to me. He asked nothing of me. There were no strings attached to his love or acceptance. Still something about him made me want to do something.

What's A Nice Jewish Girl Like Me Doing in a Place Like This?

I gingerly began to explore what Jesus might mean to me. As I did so, I took new interest in Teresa's experience. She was studying Hebrew and the Hebrew Bible in seminary, a language and text I loved. I enrolled at the same school Teresa attended, a graduate school that prepared Christians for professional ministry. I didn't plan on becoming a Christian, let alone a minister. So, what was a nice Jewish girl like me doing in a place like this?

I aced my first year. Academics, I understood. It was the extracurricular lessons that were the most foreign to me. I spent many hours in private conversations with classmates, who were steeped in life-long relationships with Jesus and with the Christian Bible.

This experience was just as intense as the new people I met

in the recovery circles. Me? I understood love of the Bible and reverent literalism. Nobody handles each jot and tittle more reverently than the Orthodox Jewish community. But these Protestants did it differently. It was more personal somehow, less cerebral. They believed God spoke to them through Jesus. This was not a Jewish way of reading the Bible.

The Call to the Ministry

The unexpected continued to unfold in my life. I kept going to the recovery circle meetings with the couches and the open, honest sharing. I remained abstinent, clean, and sober. At the same time, my newfound seminary friends continued to school me in their way of praying and understanding the Bible. The more I tried these new ways of praying, the more I found myself entering into a state of sharply heightened spiritual awareness.

I was used to being instructed in tradition and doctrine. In other words, having other people telling me what to believe. Set understandings of God, or at least set parameters of belief about God, were part of the fixed reality that had been transmitted to me. Now, with these new ways of praying, I was having direct experiences with God.

I remember the first time I read about Jesus and his miracles. I learned of his ability to heal people with his hands, his words, his power, his energy, even dirt and spittle. I was amazed that I had personally entered the world of the miraculous.

In my second year in seminary, I sensed the call to ministry. I hadn't ever expected to become a Christian. But after six years in the Orthodox Jewish community, and then straddling two worlds, I realized I was now being called to identify with this new community of Jesus-followers.

I figured I better start going to church and get baptized. I did both. It was around that same time that Doug and I parted ways, amicably. I had become a different person. So had Doug. Over the course of our short marriage, each of us had entered into emerging new identities.

I found something unsettling, though, when I began to go to church. I found a tamed version of the Jesus I had met personally. Yes, some people knew him as a rabble-rouser rabbi, but they weren't moved by his ability to interrupt the sameness of life as I was. While these folks were long-time followers of the One I had just come to know, Jesus seemed to be more of a point of comfort, not a rallying cry. He seemed to be more of a stabilizer, not a miracle-maker. Jesus had morphed into safe, predictable, nice. In my life, however, he turned things upside down: my addictions, my identity, my marriage, and my religious commitments.

> "These philosophies draw upon realities that are reflected in the Bible, yet glossed over in the church."

Same Jesus, different understandings.

A few years later, with seminary behind me, I was ordained in The United Methodist Church and entered into the ordained ministry. Like most new clergypersons, I jumped in with high expectations. I actually expected miracles.

What I found, however, over the next eleven years – serving first as an associate pastor in a vibrant, mid-sized black church, then as a co-pastor in a large white suburban church, and finally as the solo pastor in a once-larger-now-shrinking rural church – was less than miraculous. While I met warm, compassionate, and delightful people, I also experienced resistance, both to Jesus and to the ministries of the church.

In my recovery circles, I had discovered a Higher Power that breaks up fixed realities. The church's Jesus, however, seemed to reinforce them.

I'm naturally fast paced and assertive. When I first started in ministry, I was all about going out in the community and making a difference. I couldn't understand why everyone didn't feel as I did. Faced with a slower-paced and cautious church culture, I quickly began to feel an approaching burn-out.

Next Calling

As a United Methodist elder, I served as a pastor for over a decade, giving myself fully to the work of ministry. I loved the people, the preaching, the teaching, and the ability to make a difference in others' lives. What I didn't love, however, was the resistance I encountered to expanding the reach of the congregation. It was like the Jesus I met was suspect in the church. His disruptive abilities were threatening or unwelcome.

My prayer life took on a new urgency. "God, do you have anything else for me to do?"

Six months later God obliged me with an answer. Rather than leave the local church with my tail between my legs, head hung in shame about the congregation's shrinking footprint, God told me, "Your calling is not to get smaller but to get bigger." Rather than hide, it was time to be more visible. Here was Jesus sharing more authority with me, not less; more agency, not less. I felt my call was to shape larger, more empowering conversations in the church.

These conversations led me deep into the United Methodist connection. As I worked with denominational leaders, they steered me to the task of crafting next generation leadership development. Whatever I developed would need to be adaptive and innovative even as it incorporated emotional intelligence.

Helping Leaders and Congregations Dream Like Jesus

In the dozen years since leaving the pulpit, I have studied empowering principles from a variety of fields: from the

Twelve-Step model of addiction recovery to quantum physics and consciousness studies, from emotional intelligence to transformational learning and New Thought philosophy, and from hands-on healing to energy fields of the body. I have discovered a common thread that connects these disparate studies. Whether spiritual or scientific, these philosophies draw upon realities that are reflected in the Bible, yet glossed over in the church.

For instance, from the Twelve-Step model of addiction recovery and the field of emotional intelligence, I have discovered that my perceptions create my reality. Jesus once asked a lame man, "Do you want to be healed?" Because the man could envision himself whole and well, Jesus was able to affect his healing. But Jesus could only do the miraculous in partnership with the man's faith. In the same way, our attitudes set the stage for what is possible in our own lives.

Insights from quantum physics and transformational learning reinforced this "ah-ha" moment. I came to understand that our voices are imbued with the same quality of creativity inherent in God's voice. If you have ever officiated at a wedding and joined two people in holy matrimony, you've had a taste of what I mean. Our words have power.

Just as God spoke the creation into being, so, too, do we declare new realities. To be made in the image of God means we speak our world into being. At the very least, we determine our experience of it.

From various experiences, I have discovered the scientific and spiritual basis for the biblical practice of laying on of hands. Every particle in the universe – from quarks to human hearts to mountains – gives off energy. This universal energy freely flows between us and God too. The Gospel of John refers to this reality through the metaphor of the vine and the branches. "I am the vine; you are the branches" (John 15:5a NIV). What flows through both vine and branches is divine life, divine energy. It flowed in a powerful and concentrated

13

way through Jesus to the people he healed. When Jesus touched people, or they him, "power came out from him and healed all of them (Luke 6:19 NIV).

Sometimes touch wasn't even required. His observation, "Your sins are forgiven," sprung a paralyzed man from his bed (Matthew 9:5-7). Jesus simply radiated divine energy to others because, "the power of the Lord was with him to heal the sick" (Luke 5:17 NIV).

This book invites you to take the next step. Come know Jesus, and yourself, in a whole new way. It's time to meet your own power. To discover your own birthright. To claim your own blessing. It's time to dream like Jesus. And time to share that dream with the people you love, teach, and lead.

Introduction

Empowering Conversations, Empowering Results

New conversations lead to new results. Jesus understood this. He didn't recycle old complaints or harp on limiting circumstances. Rather he generated new, empowering conversations by declaring never before uttered visions. For example, "This scripture has been fulfilled in your hearing." Or, "the Kingdom of heaven is at hand."

Further, he declared that humble fishermen and corrupt tax collectors alike could heal the sick and usher the spiritually tormented into peace. Like Jesus, they, too, could share the Kingdom dream with others.

As I've explored the conversations that shape church leadership, I have realized that we in the church have been speaking from the context of decline, of focusing on what ails us. But as Albert Einstein reportedly said, "We cannot solve our problems with the same thinking we used when we created them." To rise from decline, we must use our imagination and think from the future instead of the past.

Eight years ago, I began to develop a model of leadership that generates the dynamics of renewal, rather than fixes the symptoms of decline.

Creating a Culture of Renewal®

The result is a three-year process called *Creating a Culture of Renewal*®. Since its earliest iteration in 2011, *Creating a Culture of Renewal*® has guided and empowered spiritual leaders nationwide to develop visionary ministries deeply grounded in the dreams of Jesus, and in the needs of their communities. *Creating a Culture of Renewal*® is a group coaching process which establishes a high-trust, high-accountability context in the group. During the three-year process, we train mixed groups of laity, clergy, and denominational executives.

In year one, "Congregational Intelligence," leaders apply principles of emotional intelligence to the life of their committee, congregation, or region. They discover the unconscious communications and unspoken messages that conspire to keep their ministries small and stuck. Along the way, they grow in confidence and self-awareness as they practice people-reading and communication skills, and prepare their people to engage in a Jesus-like dream.

Throughout the second year, church leaders cultivate "Leadership Smarts." They name and reframe their limiting beliefs, transferring them from the fear column to the faith column. Like an ever-changing kaleidoscope, stubborn fears give way to courage and freedom. Parameters of seemingly fixed reality rearrange themselves into newfound skill and poise. These leaders discover a surprising truth: quite often it's the very things they themselves are afraid of saying, trying, or doing that prevents change from occurring. Freed up from the constraints of the past, they create Jesus-like dreams that are both inspiring and risky. The only kind that make a true difference.

In the third year, "Culture Shift," church leaders begin to master the elusive skill necessary to get and keep others on board with a vision, and to fully implement the vision. They also develop a team so that implementation of the vision isn't limited by the amount of empty space in their calendar or the room on their to-do list. Because all the work doesn't fall on their shoulders, these leaders can create a sustainable culture shift in the self-identity, focus, and process of the congregation.

A vibrant graduate community of faculty and mentors has caught this vision and together we lead and empower a nationwide network of cohorts. This year alone our team served one thousand church leaders and members across the United States.

The hard-won wisdom of the *Creating a Culture of Renewal*® process has been distilled into this volume.

Take the DARE

I wrote *Dream Like Jesus*® for spiritual leaders in the United Methodist Church and beyond: clergy and laity who are passionate about the gospel, yet deeply concerned about the future of the church. My intention is to inspire and equip you to dare to live out your callings anew. *Dream Like Jesus*® gives you a four-part process to envision and enact a Kingdom-oriented future for your congregations and communities based on the acronym DARE, which stands for Dream, Align, Realize, and Expand.

Part one of *Dream Like Jesus*® is about the rise and fall of Jesus' big dream for the world. In chapter one, I describe the nature of Jesus' big dream and how his followers have tended, and sometimes neglected, his big dream over the centuries. In chapter two, I demonstrate how the US church of the twentieth and twenty-first century has all but forgotten his dream. As a result, many congregations have slid and lurched into decline. In chapter three, I identify eight noticeable symptoms that reliably signal a congregation's downward spiral.

Part two begins the DARE model. First, I address how to

DREAM like Jesus. In chapter four, I demonstrate that Jesus has authorized spiritual leaders like you to dream big. In chapter five, I reveal the five surprising elements of a Jesus-like dream. In chapter six, I show you how to create your own Jesus-like dream.

Part three continues the DARE model. Next comes how to ALIGN others to the dream. In chapter seven, I teach you how to get your congregation on board with the new dream. In chapter eight, I walk you through the reasons and rationale you will need to help people navigate change. In chapter nine, I explore the positive power of negative pushback.

Part four also continues the DARE model. This step shows you how to REALIZE the dream. In chapter ten, I walk you through strategic steps to make the dream reality. Chapter eleven gives you the push needed to move your dream forward. In chapter twelve, you discover the importance of acknowledging and celebrating all that you have accomplished.

Part five completes the DARE model. Here you discover how to EXPAND the dream. In chapters thirteen, fourteen, and fifteen, you'll read about how congregations intensify their impact, how you'll amplify partnership with God, and how you and your people's faith will be magnified, all when you dare to take on a Jesus-like dream.

In part six, you'll see how the future is now yours. In chapter sixteen, I empower you to foster and cultivate new dreams. In chapter seventeen, I suggest Jesus' next big dream for the world and demonstrate how you can begin to lead with this vision now. Finally, in chapter eighteen, I conclude with provocative thoughts for the future.

Will you DARE to dream like Jesus? Let's get going! The future awaits.

CHAPTER ONE

Jesus' Big Dream
for the World

Jesus' existence was grounded in dreams, both the sleeping and waking kind. Were it not for the power of dreams, Joseph, Jesus' father, would have divorced Mary, his mother (Matthew 1:10). Herod in his paranoia would have detained the Magi (Matthew 2:11) and later, in a murdering madness, would have killed the toddler Jesus (Matthew 2:16). As it was, another dream warned Joseph to take his fledgling family to seek refuge in Egypt (Matthew 1:13). Still another dream signaled the danger had passed, and they could once again return to Israel (Matthew 2:19). Each of these dreams impacted Jesus' first years.

While the dreams of Jesus' early years ensured his survival, a different kind of dream – a waking dream – steered his adult years. Being a visionary, Jesus dreamed big dreams. He envisioned a world in which the meek would inherit the earth, the poor in spirit would be blessed, and the grieving would be comforted. He dreamed of a world where people would love each other with the same generous spirit with which he loved. Jesus imagined a world where his diverse followers would unite as one.

Even now, each of his big dreams stretches the imagination and kindles the heart. I believe his biggest, most compelling dream was this: "Thy Kingdom come, thy will be done, on earth as it is in heaven." This dream was so big that it shaped his entire ministry. It accompanied his every moment.

The reason Jesus was sent, he explained, "is to go and proclaim the good news of the Kingdom of God" (Luke 4:43). He taught about this Kingdom, preached about it, and told many a story about it. Most memorably, of course, he lifted the Kingdom up in prayer. In fact, every time we pray the Lord's Prayer, we are recalling and reaffirming Jesus' big dream.[1]

What was this Kingdom? Volumes have been written from every perspective imaginable, ranging from the mystical to the practical, the psychological to the sociological, the scientific to the spiritual, the ecological to the economic, as well as those that draw from both Jewish sources and Gnostic Gospels. In particular, I have appreciated *Wisdom Jesus: Transforming Heart and Mind – a New Perspective on Christ and His Message* by Cynthia Bourgeault,[2] *The Universal Christ: How a Forgotten Reality Can Change Everything We See, Hope For and Believe*, by Richard Rohr,[3] *The Kingdom Within: The Inner Meaning of Jesus' Sayings* by John A. Sanford;[4] *Quantum Theology, Theological Implications of the New Physics* by Diarmuid O'Murchu,[5] and *Short Stories by Jesus* by Amy Jill-Levine.[6]

While these varied resources have expanded my thinking, simply put, I believe Jesus envisioned an earth that fully reflected the goodness of heaven (Matthew 6:10). He dreamed that all the love, light, beauty, bounty, humor, harmony, acceptance and forgiveness, creativity and magnificence, unity and inclusion, joy and justice, peace and plenty we associate with God, would be manifest here on earth. And not just manifested around us, but first and foremost within us.

Jesus' dream goes by another name: The Kingdom of God, or in the Gospel of Matthew, the Kingdom of heaven.[7] This Kingdom realm was the subject of much of his teaching and preaching. Despite Matthew's use of the term "heaven," Jesus wasn't talking about life after death. He was talking about his dream of vibrant, abundant life before death. Matthew's Gospel, however, aligned with Jewish sensitivity to the third commandment, "Thou shalt not take the name of the LORD thy God in vain."[8] Thus, the word heaven is substituted for God.[9] So, whether Jesus called this realm the Kingdom of God or the Kingdom of heaven, he was pointing to one and the same desire: that we experience what Jesus did – an earthly existence suffused with the sacred and permeated by the presence of God. Jesus dreamed of nothing less than that we experience ourselves as one with the Source of all Being.

> **"I am not so smitten by Jesus' Kingdom dream as to believe all expressions of it have been holy."**

Another note about language. The biblical term "Kingdom" refers back to the monarchical period in Jewish history. It is carried forth in to the New Testament and extra-biblical Jewish sources. In the US, as much as we are intrigued with all things royal, we do not live in a monarchy. The term feels somewhat foreign on our tongues. Additionally, male-specific language is no longer considered inclusive. New terms have arisen that capture the essence of Jesus' message such as the Reign and Realm of God, Kin(g)dom and Beloved Community. While I find all these additional terms perfectly acceptable, I am partial to the term Kingdom because Jesus was. Nevertheless, I'll use the term Kingdom when I'm quoting scripture or speaking of Jesus, and a mix of the other terms including Kingdom, when I'm speaking about current manifestations of Jesus' dream.

Jesus' Kingdom dream was so powerful that it gave rise to an entire world. Before Jesus shared his dream, there were no disciples, no apostles, no Gospels, and no church. Christianity flowed out of the generative power of Jesus' big dream. Reality shifted because Jesus declared his vision of the Kingdom, and an entirely new world emerged, founded on this dream.

That's the power of a vision. It changes reality. It re-arranges old circumstances as it calls forth new structures, generates new identities, summons new resources, and draws in new people. A powerful vision speaks new possibilities into being.

Jesus introduced people to a fresh, visionary power in the world. His own life-giving dreams and reality-shifting prayers resulted in breathtaking miracles. Just ask Jairus' daughter, Peter's mother-in-law, or Lazarus after he was called out from the grave. You yourself may be a living example of just such a miracle.

What's striking to me is that Jesus didn't hoard this power. He freely taught others how to exercise it. First, he taught his followers and students – his disciples – how to harness and use this power. During the three years they spent with him, they observed how he thought and how he prayed. They watched how he taught and soaked up what he believed. They watched him engage paralyzed, hurting, desperate people and they noted the way he interacted with others. They listened to the way he phrased things. They were privy to his miracles and glimpsed his inner relationship with God. Jesus showed them all this because they would not only be his disciples, but his apostles.

Eventually, Jesus sent them out on their own to do the very things he had done. For instance, when the disciples pointed out that the thousands of people who had come out to hear Jesus' teaching were hungry, Jesus wasn't interested in sending them away to find food. "You give them something to eat," he said. You may think of Jesus as the one who multiplied loaves and fishes. Yet, it wasn't until the bits of bread and fish passed through the hands of his friends and students that the food began to multiply. When Peter asked Jesus if he too could walk on water, Jesus said, "Sure! Come on out and meet me." When the disciples questioned Jesus about why they couldn't rid a young man of demons, Jesus filled in the blanks for them (Matthew 17:14-20). It was simply a matter of more faith, but not some impossible-to-attain faith. Rather, Jesus pointed to the power of God which already existed within them. With practice, they were able to tap into that "unsuspected inner resource" and to consistently do the very things Jesus did.

> **"I believe Jesus envisioned an earth that fully reflected the glory of heaven."**

Once they learned how to exercise this visionary power, the disciples and apostles wholeheartedly embraced it, and then turned the world upside down with it. Not only did they heal, preach, and proclaim, they gathered thousands of followers, set up communities in far-flung places, and oversaw the development of structures that allowed the church to grow and expand throughout the known world.

But this exponential expansion didn't stop with that first generation of disciples and apostles. Over the centuries, new generations of disciples and apostles caught Jesus' dream: "Thy Kingdom come, thy will be done, on earth as it is in heaven." They, too, exercised the creative power to speak new realities into being. Their visions gave rise to new Christian communities throughout the world beginning after the fall of Jerusalem in the year 70 AD. The Desert Mothers and Fathers cultivated prayer and meditation practices that flowered in the second century and continue to bloom to this day. Ecclesial authorities commissioned the construction of soaring cathedrals that touched the heavens beginning in the Constantinian period and continuing through the

Renaissance. The Catholic Church, often mistakenly accused of suppressing the intellect, was the guardian of almost all intellectual endeavors in the Middle Ages. During this time, it gave generous support to the development of math, academia, and the sciences. Twin gifts sanctioned by the Church – reason and faith – combined to create a culture of innovation we now take for granted. Inventions such as spectacles, horseshoes, and stirrups were part of this creative advance. What was then called "natural philosophy" and today is known as study of the natural world, got its start at that time.[10] All of this was an outgrowth of a Kingdom consciousness.

The Middle Ages also witnessed the church's support of higher education in the eleventh and twelfth centuries along with the rise of universities. Classical music found its start in the Middle Ages, first grounded in monophonic Gregorian Chant, which set the prayers of the Divine offices to music. In centuries to come, more polyphonic melodies emerged from the plainchant, often commissioned by the Church.[11] In the fifteenth century on, painters such as El Greco and da Vinci created stirring works of religious art which continue to fire the imagination hundreds of years later. Each of these new realities expanded the reach and expression of the Kingdom.

Faith and reason combined once again to undergird social justice movements, liberation theologies, and the overthrowing of tyrants from the seventeenth century on. The abolition of slavery in the US and women's right to vote at the turn of the nineteenth century, countless civil rights movements in the US and around the world in the 1900s, acts of goodness and kindness of every sort, and in almost every time and place the care and feeding of orphans and hungry children have all been inspired by Jesus' visionary dream: "Thy Kingdom come, thy will be done, on earth as it is in heaven."

Even as expressions of Jesus' dream have multiplied, so have his followers. At last count, the original twelve friends and followers of Jesus have evolved into a sprawling complex of thirty-three thousand Christian denominations. His unaffiliated fans spill out beyond that. Not to mention Jesus-admirers who belong to other religious bodies.

Of course, I am not so smitten by Jesus' Kingdom dream as to believe all expressions of it have been holy. I describe in great detail in *The Jew Named Jesus* the Church's bloody history of violence against Jews and Judaism. As I note in that book, these grotesque disfigurations of the Kingdom ideal arise from a mistaken notion of a good Christian Jesus who stood against bad faithless Jews.

This same misunderstanding of Jesus today translates into an endless litany of faithless opponents against whom faithful Christians believe they must stand against in order to stand with Jesus. Thus, we have anti-Muslim, anti-gay, and anti-immigrant campaigns carried out in the name of Jesus. Not to mention anti-progressive, anti-conservative, anti-Democratic and anti-Republican campaigns, and anything else someone thinks Jesus would disapprove.

All this bad history notwithstanding, in this book, I focus on the life-giving aspects of the Kingdom ideal. After all, what would this world be without Jesus' dream? "Thy Kingdom come, thy will be done, on earth as it is in heaven" has compelled the creation of heretofore unknown realities and brand-new institutions since it was first uttered. Its manifestation has fulfilled the deeper meaning of the word salvation. While salvation has been equated with a spiritual conversion experience, in the Hebrew Bible – Jesus' Bible – the word salvation conveys a multi-dimensional wholeness.[12] Salvation is a form of communal well-being that includes peace and safety, freedom to worship, material prosperity, health, and a blessed connection to God, the source of life itself.

Given the power of this dream, and all it has inspired over the course of centuries, it begs the questions: Why isn't Jesus' big dream fueling the growth of churches in the Western world today? And why isn't Christianity thriving in these places?

CHAPTER TWO
The Church in Decline

Even though Christians love and emulate a visionary dreamer whose dream reshaped the arc of history, congregations that bear Jesus' name are struggling. Rather than thriving, many of these congregations fight to survive. Some of them have already given up the fight. It's no secret that many Christian denominations in the United States – from mainline Protestants to Evangelicals – have been in decline for up to half a century.[13] While religious groups that encourage large families or dissuade members from using birth control are still growing, even their rate of growth has slowed.[14] Across the religious landscape, formal religious practice is no longer the center of communal life. A recently released Gallup poll confirms that church membership in the US has plummeted over the last twenty years.[15] Why is that?

Those in the mainline Protestant world have rehearsed the answer many times, and it sounds something like this. Our churches would be full again if . . .

- Parents would just stop taking their kids to soccer practice on Sunday mornings.

- Church buildings had more curb appeal.

- Preachers were better.

- Society wasn't so individualistic or permissive or sinful.

- Young people would come to church.

27

- Families would tithe.

- Schedules weren't so darn busy.

- Newcomers would do things the way we already like to do things.

- The NFL, the PGA, and the MLB didn't televise on Sunday.

- Members didn't spend their weekends camping or golfing.

Maybe parents, church buildings, preachers, young people, families, schedules, new members, professional sports, and nature are the cause. But I don't think so.

These are excuses, not explanations. Yes, the world is changing. Social and religious commentators Phyllis Tickle and Diana Butler Bass have elucidated those changes in their ground-breaking writings.[16] Tickle wrote about the five-hundred-year rummage sale in which the church must sort through its beliefs, tossing aside what no longer suits while retaining what still fits.

Butler Bass imagined Christianity after religion and the power of faith grounded in earthy practices. Churches that are weird, messy, and fresh have all attempted to keep up with a world that is hot, flat, and crowded.[17] Meanwhile, younger generations simply don't join or trust organizations like older generations do.

At the same time the Western world is increasingly less religious, it has also become increasingly more spiritual. It seems like society has outpaced the church in its willingness to visibly embrace a miracle-mindset. You can even take "A Course in Miracles." Hundreds of thousands across the world do.

Caught between these two competing forces – the breakdown of religious affiliation and the increase in spiritual self-identification – the underlying cause of the decline of the church takes on new clarity. The church is in decline because we have stopped dreaming like Jesus.

Abraham Joshua Heschel, the noted Jewish thinker once

wrote, "It is customary to blame secular science and anti-religious philosophy for the eclipse of religion in modern society. It would be more honest to blame religion for its own defeats. Religion declined not because it was refuted, but because it became irrelevant, dull, oppressive, and insipid...When faith becomes an heirloom rather than a living fountain, when religion speaks only in the name of authority rather than with the voice of compassion, its message becomes meaningless."[18]

Although Heschel was writing about Judaism, the same can be said of Christianity. Take, for example, the crises around clergy sex abuse scandals convulsing the Roman Catholic Church and the Southern Baptist Convention. These institutions are scripting their own defeats. The United Methodist Church is not immune from self-sabotage. Norms related to human sexuality and biblical interpretation are at the center of implosions in this denomination, too. At a special called session of The United Methodist Church's global decision-making body, delegates to the 2019 General Conference voted to retain and reinforce traditional views on appropriate expressions of human sexuality, adding punitive measures to ensure this point of view. While a majority in the US favored a more nuanced and inclusive approach to embracing varied cultural and theological stances in this country, alliances with more conservative African, Asian, and Eastern European churches won out.

Was this act an affirmation of conservative-minded readings of the Bible, an act of outright discrimination, or perhaps "less an act of exclusion than the result of the inability of that church's internal polity to keep pace with its flourishing ministry among L.G.B.T. Americans?"[19] Whatever the intent, ironically, love has become a wedge issue.

Trust in institutions, already waning, is now declining precipitously. In the midst of massive cultural change, the church has gone into shock, defensively operating from a reactionary mode. Churches see themselves as the victims of change, not agents of transformation.

But even in the midst of a rapidly changing culture, I believe

Jesus and his dream are crucial. Churches shrink and die if his life-giving dream doesn't lead the way.

McKenzie agrees. She pastors a church in the North Carolina Piedmont. "The people I have served in rural areas struggle to see themselves as having the potential to be spiritual giants," she observed to me. I know what she means, I have seen this, too. Yet in my experience, it's not just rural areas. People in urban areas limit their spiritual capacities in much the same way. McKenzie agrees with this as well. "The bigger biblical things like participating in the redemptive work of God, the sense of oneness with God, dreaming that we can change the future – these concepts are all reserved for the 'big' spiritual people."

Guess what? We all have spiritual capacities beyond our wildest dreams.

Here's a thought. What if the problem isn't the people in the pews – rural or urban – but the way spiritual leaders lead them? I suggest that churches have forgotten the power Jesus gives his disciples. (I'm not talking about the power to bring back the supposed good old days of the 1950s or 1960s. Those days are gone. They're not coming back.) I'm talking about the power to declare a new and better future for everyone. Yes, the church has stopped dreaming like Jesus. Or maybe it hasn't dared to try.

I believe most of church decline is due to lack of a bold vision, a vision that reflects Jesus' dream of heaven on earth.[20] Instead of pursuing God-sized dreams or a Kingdom consciousness, the Church has gotten sidetracked, sucked into a survival mentality. As one pastor noted to me, "To be little with God, is to be little for God."

The church has forgotten that Jesus said your thoughts, your prayers, and your faith make you unstoppable. "[I]f you have faith as small as a mustard seed, you can say to this mountain, 'Move from here to there,' and it will move" (Matthew 17:20). And, "Whatever you ask for in prayer, believe that you have received it, and it will be yours" (Matthew 11:24). Nothing is impossible for you (Matthew 17:20b; Luke 17:6; Matthew 21:21, Mark 11:23). In fact, "all things are possible for those that believe" (Mark 9:23).

The church has forgotten that to be made in the image and likeness of God means that just as God calls into existence "the things that do not (yet) exist," (Romans 4:17), so can you, by the power of your word. The church has forgotten that Jesus has given her the keys to the Kingdom, and with them the power of choice. In Matthew, Jesus quotes a popular *targum,* or interpretation, of classical Judaism which affirms the human responsibility to choose: "Whatever you bind on earth is bound in heaven, and whatever you loose on earth is loosed in heaven."[21] Jesus affirms your power of choice saying, in essence, "Look, when it comes to matters of interpretation, you, the church, get to decide. You work it out; heaven will go along." Here again, the term heaven is a substitute for God.

While the church is busy duking out finer points of the Law – like Torah teachers and Pharisees who conscientiously tithed their spices yet avoided weightier matters of Torah living such as justice, mercy, and faithfulness[22] – scores of people are leaving the church, believing that the church's purpose is to judge people, not to free them, and to limit them, not to empower them.

Interestingly, thousands initially sought out Jesus precisely because of the empowerment he offered. Now, sadly, millions have left because they no longer sense that freedom in the church. They turn away from the doors of the church thinking the church is irrelevant, hypocritical, and hypercritical, precisely the opposite of what I believe Jesus would have wanted.

I think back on the freedom and love Jesus offered me. When he told me, "I understand you, I love you, and I accept you," that was pure gift, precisely because there were no strings attached. His words empowered me rather than constrained me. Truthfully, he didn't have to share any of that with me. At the time I wasn't a Christian, nor did I ever intend to be. Jesus and I weren't friends. His unexpected involvement in my life shifted my awareness of what was possible. It started a new chapter, a new dream, in my life.

Given Jesus' desire to share his power, what surprises me

is that the church, the people gathered in his name, act like his power and empowerment is no longer available. Love: yes, power: no. Even more shocking is that leaders of the church are often unaware or unwilling to tap into the transformational power Jesus once authorized his disciples and apostles to exercise. As a result, churches lose their ability to empower great good in the world.

In this book, I want to upend the church's well-rehearsed reasons and excuses that conspire to keep it small and stuck. The church doesn't suffer from too high expectations. Just the opposite. You expect too little and dream too small. I want to equip you to dream like Jesus again! To set your course by the star of Jesus' dream of heaven on earth.

The moment the church dares to dream like Jesus again, a brand-new chapter opens up. Not only for the church, but for the communities you serve and the world as a whole. In this new chapter of the Kingdom dream, it will no longer be institution-building that defines the Christian movement. Rather, I predict that the Kingdom dream will manifest in the transformation of human consciousness, as we grow in courage and ability to co-create with God.

As we step into our new-found abilities to co-create with God, we will see new, inspiring social and spiritual movements take place. New forms of beloved community, compassion, and caring will emerge. Divides will be bridged. Unconditional love will be ascendant.

Before we talk about this next phase of the Kingdom, however, let's take a look at the current state of affairs in your ministry setting. In the next chapter, I'll introduce you to the eight symptoms of a church in decline. These are the symptoms of a church that has not dared to dream like Jesus. Without an inspiring Kingdom-oriented vision to guide it, decline is inevitable. See if you recognize yourself or your people in these pages.

CHAPTER THREE

Eight Symptons
of a Church Without Vision

At Shepherd of the Hills Church, it's been a long time since the cries of children interrupted worship. That's okay with this aging congregation. Although they miss younger people, they appreciate less commotion. If only they could get some responsible families, they're sure things would look up. They want the pastor to recruit them. But he's gotten busy lately, bogged down in church meetings that seem to go nowhere.

This congregation has tried to start a "Bring a Friend to Worship" Sunday. But newcomers get scared off by the appeals to give, and the red ink in the bulletin. Meanwhile the pews thin out, and a steady stream of funerals keep the pastor hopping. Worship used to include several unknown faces. Not anymore, but at least now everyone knows each other. Lots of time to pray for each other, and to keep the love flowing.

On the surface, this church sounds pretty normal. But dig down a bit and you'll find a church in decline. This is a church with an alarming state of affairs; it has no dream other than to survive. Churches like this develop a bevy of problems. In fact, I've identified eight quite distinct symptoms.

In my work with congregations, these are the eight decline dynamics I have seen repeated again and again:

- shrinking numbers

- problem people

- stagnant giving

- listless worship

- gutless prayer

- bait and switch evangelism

- insulated focus

- dead-end decision-making.

These dynamics are reliable indicators of a church operating without a vision.

Symptom 1: Shrinking Numbers

Let's start with shrinking numbers. In a church operating without a Jesus-like dream to guide it, not only do ministries stall and shrink, but Bible studies that once propelled new ministries now reinforce age separations and static worldviews. I've seen it time and again. Instead of the dramatic stories of the Bible generating new actions and attitudes, they become the focus for generational-based cliques. Ultimately, the numbers of people participating in classes go down due to poor health, moves, disability, and death.

But it's not just Bible studies that shrink. In a church without a vision, worship attendance plateaus, drops, and ultimately dwindles. As worship attendance declines, so do the professions of faith. Burials outpace baptisms. This accelerating trend of adding to the "great cloud of witnesses" is visible across the Protestant spectrum, from United Methodists to Southern Baptists.[23] Compound this trend with relocations, transfers to other churches or denominations, dwindling belief, and sense of belonging, and the numbers drop for all sorts of reasons. While shrinking numbers should catch your attention, that's not all that happens in a vision-less church.

Symptom 2: Problem People

The second symptom of decline in churches which don't dream like Jesus is an increase in problem people. In observations made by George Bullard,[24] as a congregation's ranks thin out, the rate and depth of conflicts increase. The loyal remnant – those who remain after others have left – tend to be territorial, wielding a firm grip on day-to-day operations. All the while reminding others of how things used to be or how they are done now. While institutional memory can create helpful touchstones in charting a fresh course into the future, it's not so helpful when the footbridge to said future has toll bridges along the way, demanding the payment of heavy fees for proceeding. This longing for the church to pick up its old ways once more can cause stability-seeking people to resist the future and the inevitable changes it holds. Even when those changes promise better outcomes. Fresh ideas are treated as suspect, especially if they appear risky or costly. The drive to conserve resources fortifies resistance.

Miss DeLynda, the former Lay Leader of a once vibrant congregation, ran up against this exact problem. Passionate and decisive, this feisty seventy-something year old had been sounding the alarm for years: "We need to make some new decisions here, people. And fast! Otherwise, we're going to die." Her words were met with squirming silence and the occasional eye roll.

Even though others secretly suspected she was right, the leadership of the church dragged its feet. They were reluctant to risk negative feedback from the changes she suggested like shifting the worship times, insisting on more topically relevant sermons, an updated nursery, and more engaging worship with better music. She delivered tough information the same way she liked to receive it: quickly and directly. Her fellow worshipers were more indirect and cautious in their communication style. Convinced that none of them cared about the church anyway, she left in anger and frustration when she didn't get the response she was seeking.

While Miss DeLynda was spot-on with many of her insights and suggestions, her way of handling disappointment and inaction didn't help. Even as she tried to bring a solution, she herself, became identified as a problem. The point is, both cautious, reluctant, harmony-seekers, and impatient, straight-talking doers can generate conflict in a church that operates without a guiding vision.

As a general rule of thumb, conflict increases as the pool of shared resources decreases and as the realization settles in that the good ol' days really are over. It's like squeezing lighter fluid on a smoldering fire. With the exit of passionate leaders like Miss DeLynda, new leaders are in short supply. Often those that step forward are second-tier choices.

Symptom 3: Stagnant Giving

The third symptom of decline is stagnant giving. As a church valiantly plods on without a vision, the existence of the church itself becomes the focus of giving. A church I attend features a chart in its bulletin that highlights worship attendance, giving figures, and gains and losses for the month and year. Those figures aren't as compelling as a Kingdom-oriented vision. In fact, unless this chart is balanced with a vision that is equally visible, the data itself become a self-fulfilling prophesy. Without a vision to chart a course into the future, giving is increasingly concentrated in the hands of a few. These still-generous givers remember a previous vision, a former favorite pastor, or a more vibrant chapter in the congregation's past. They feel it's their duty to keep that memory of church alive.

If you're serving a congregation like this, have you noticed how as the base of givers shrinks, you yourself tend to become more cautious, more solicitous? It's human nature to consider how your sermons, decisions, and dreams may sound to your congregation's remaining benefactors. The last thing you want is to lose your most generous givers to conflict, not to mention age-related absences or death. Consequently, you tiptoe around bigger issues, afraid to be prophetic, risk too much, or say something out of turn lest a large contributor get offended and withdraw their financial support. It's one hell of a scary, stressful way to lead.

Here's the thing, though. Without your willingness to truly lead with a Jesus-like dream, the ministry suffers anyway. As you'll see in this section, the most basic elements of church life wither without a vision to undergird them. When you don't lead with a vision, your people won't be inspired to give generously, which then magnifies the fear of lack of money. This fear crystallizes into the perception that there is no money, regardless of the size of the budget. Money becomes synonymous with fear and stress. The church, supposed bastion of the Jesus who gives life abundantly, operates from a scarcity model in which miracles are rare and the word prosperity is frowned upon. Money seems to be the main problem, rather than a mere symptom.

Symptom 4: Listless Worship

The fourth symptom of a church without a Jesus-like dream is listless worship. You've seen it, haven't you? In a church devoid of Kingdom dreams, worship meanders. Sunday services gather no steam, build no momentum, and deliver no promise. When weekly worship is disconnected from a larger purpose, your people sense it, too.

I learned this the hard way. Both Sunday morning services were over at the large suburban church that I co-pastored at the time. The church had a terrific music program, which attracted a lot of worshipers. But vision was harder to come by. Jesse, an astute worshiper from the second service, remarked to me that Sunday, "It's like we're throwing a party, but the guest of honor never shows up." That's a church without a vision. At its best, worship just misses the mark. At its worst, it stagnates, suffocating new life.

Worship can either be the life-blood of a thriving church which dreams like Jesus or it can be a painful reminder that any Jesus-like dreams have long since evaporated. Vision is the thread that holds everything together. Why are we so drawn to the beatitudes in the Sermon on the Mount? It was Jesus' astonishing worldview. Why does the Lord's Prayer so engage us? I believe it's the inherent power of vision in the prayer. When you dare to build on the dreams of Jesus, inspiration makes more guest appearances in worship.

Symptom 5: Gutless Prayer

Gutless prayer is the fifth symptom of a church in decline. In most of the churches I visit, three main prayer concerns loop on auto-repeat: health, travel, and the military. While there's nothing wrong with these particular concerns, they reveal your congregation's limited focus and unsteady theological foundation. They also point to three limiting perspectives in your church.

First, gutless prayer indicates that the Kingdom of God is mostly concerned with and can have the greatest impact on one's personal life: health and travels. In this case, the Kin(g)dom isn't about connection. In fact, it doesn't transcend concerns of the individual. Societal dynamics become controversial. While John Sanford's classic volume, *The Kingdom Within,* details the Kingdom's positive impact on your individual personhood, it's not limited to your personal life. When you treat it like that, you limit the sense of the Kin(g)dom, diminishing its scope and impact. Then, you shy away from lifting up systemic injustices or the people most impacted by them. If the Beloved Community doesn't include concerns of the community, is it really the dream of Jesus?

Second, a repetitive prayer focus on the military, to the exclusion of other elements of human life, speaks to syncretism of God's Kingdom with America the Great. Many churches cannot separate what it means to be a citizen of the Kingdom and a citizen of the US. Again, my friend McKenzie reflected on this, "I grew up in a church, and serve one, where God's Kingdom and the United States are inseparable. Part of my vision as a pastor is to help the church separate herself from being die-hard American and embrace being the Kin(g)dom here in America." That distinction is lost in many congregations. Let me say that I believe in our democracy and in democratic institutions. I appreciate the economic opportunities afforded by capitalism. I'm not here to tear either one down. Yet God's promise and power of the Kin(g)dom far exceeds government and economy. It can work through them but it's not equivalent to them.

The third limitation that gutless prayer points to is the lack of moral imagination. The treasury of biblical wisdom declares unequivocally that even the most courageous, outrageous prayers are welcome. "Ask and it will be given to you; seek and you will find; knock and the door will be opened to you" (Matthew 7:7 NIV). Is there anything unclear about that? "For everyone who asks receives; the one who seeks finds; and to the one who knocks, the door will be opened" (Matthew 7:8 NIV). The bottom line is this: prayer is a powerful way to call forth new realities. Jesus affirmed this idea many times. "I tell you, you can pray for anything, and if you believe that you've received it, it will be yours" (Matthew 18:19). All it takes is two people to agree on something for the request to be acted upon (Matthew 18:19, NLT). So, what's with the gutless prayer?

Many congregations say they want more young people, but you can't tell by the prayers they offer. Concerns of young people are rarely lifted up. The sense of Beloved Community promised by Jesus' Kingdom dream is limited to who is already in the congregation.

The pastoral prayer reveals which congregations are playing it safe, and which are playing full out. Although my United Methodist faith tradition discourages betting, I'm willing to wager that there is positive correlation between congregations which offer up bland, repetitive prayers and those that lack a Jesus-like dream. The truth is, our gutless prayers don't ask as much as God is willing to offer. They're not big enough, curious enough, or courageous enough to merit risk, or to call forth miraculous answers. It's as though you're praying, "My safe and secure Kingdom come, my little will be done!"

Symptom 6: Bait and Switch Evangelism

The sixth symptom of a church without a vision is bait and switch evangelism, much like the illegal practice of getting shoppers in the door by baiting them with a tantalizing, yet nonexistent, deal. Then, once the shopper comes to the store (or clicks through a website), she can't find the advertised deal. Instead, the bargain she expected has been switched for a lower-quality or higher-priced substitute.

This sort of fraudulent practice is not confined to retail and online shopping. It is practiced in the church as well. Congregations bemoan a lack of generational diversity and rightly aim to engage younger people. However, most church evangelism campaigns, if they exist at all, are poorly disguised attempts to get young people involved again so that they shoulder the church financially, or even take over leadership. That's bait and switch. Financial support and leadership are important, but that duplicity is going about it the wrong way. It is best elicited by a daring dream, not manipulated by fear or desperation.

Jeremy Smith, a savvy pastor and blogger, once noted, "The church thinks that the young people will save the church, but actually the young people want to save the world. If we can show them that the young people can save the world through the church, then young people will gladly be a part of the church."

Often when young people do wander into a church – which can take a fair amount of courage on their part if they haven't been raised in church – they are met with a divisive, if unspoken, critique: You young people don't care like we do, you don't see church being as important as we do. The truth is, they probably don't. But with that sort of welcome, it's no wonder young people take their spiritual hunger and compassionate hearts elsewhere, rather than partner with an inhospitable church.

If you're looking for people to fill an administrative spot or contribute to the offering plate, have the decency to say that to people you are inviting to church. If you actually want to introduce people to a vibrant community of faith that will make a difference in their lives, then have the decency to be that. Otherwise, it's bait and switch evangelism.

Not sure how? Keep reading. Becoming this sort of community of faith takes a Jesus-like dream to guide and transform it.

Symptom 7: Insulated Focus

The seventh dynamic of decline is an insulated focus. When a congregation has an insulated focus, it doesn't turn its gaze outward to the community around it, as John Wesley once did when he said, "All the world's my parish." Instead, the sole focus of the congregation is the worshiping congregation.

You know your congregation has an insulated focus if the makeup of the congregation doesn't reflect that of the neighborhood around it. For instance, if there's a mismatch between the generations, ethnicity, income, and/or education in your neighborhood and in your congregation, your congregation likely has an insulated focus. Do people from the neighborhood attend the church and participate in providing for its ministries? Do people from the congregation mix with the community or socialize locally? If the answer is no, your congregation has an insulated focus.

If the one exception is that your congregation offers emergency financial or food assistance, you may still have an insulated focus. While there's nothing wrong with providing stop-gap measures, this sort of ministry provides but a limited aperture. It yields a distorted snapshot of the community around you. In fact, this may be the sort of ministry that actually prevents real community from forming. The Kingdom dream implies give and take, not just give. For instance, Jesus didn't only heal, cast out demons, and dispense teaching. He also received. Without his network of friends – from Peter and his mother, to Martha, Mary, and Lazarus – Jesus would have had no place to lay his head. A Jesus-like dream will always propel you deeper into the community where both giving and receiving are required.

Symptom 8: Dead-End Decision-Making

The eighth and final dynamic of churches without a Jesus-like dream is dead-end decision-making. A Jesus-like dream demands a certain sense of adventure, wonder, and curiosity about what is possible. It requires seeing if the water will actually support you as you step out of the boat. It needs people who are willing to move a decision forward without having every eventuality covered first. In other words, it requires faith in the unknown. Maintaining the status quo demands none of that. Good enough is good enough. Dead-end decision-making is the result. With no sense of urgency to embody risky faith, decisions get delayed or pushed off the agenda.

Several years back, I was leading a packed workshop at a leadership development day for lay leaders. As we talked about dead-end decision-making, a fellow stood up and confessed, "Yeah, I've delayed decisions on purpose in meetings. In fact, I've delayed decisions for two or three months in a row."

"Then what happened?" I asked.

"Eventually we forgot about it and it went away." The room erupted in wry laughter, heads nodding as self-awareness dawned.

When dead-end decision-making is at play, caution elbows faith out of the way as it climbs into the driver's seat and shifts into low gear. The work of the church lurches forward hesitantly, like a car with the emergency brake on. Only safe ministries that are sure to work are considered. If initiatives do fail, the leader is blamed. Then pet projects, which Robert Schnase has aptly named "shadow missions," such as preservation of the building or maintaining customs of the past, take precedence over untried ministries.

Without a vision to guide decision-making, leaders and members have no clear criteria by which to evaluate options. Decision-making flounders, hijacked by potential concerns. Caution coupled with a concern for stability, rather than bold action grounded in exuberant trust, wins out.

Look around your church. How many of these eight dynamics of decline do you deal with?

- shrinking numbers
- problem people
- stagnant giving
- listless worship
- gutless prayer
- bait and switch evangelism
- insulated focus
- dead-end decision-making.

In my experience, the longer you wait to address these deadly dynamics, the more embedded they'll become and the harder they'll be to dislodge.

Decline is like an auto-immune disorder in which the body attacks itself. Early in my journey of recovery from addiction, I was diagnosed with fibromyalgia. Fibromyalgia is a form of soft tissue arthritis. Inflammation in the muscles around the joints caused my joints to ache all the time. Fibromyalgia pain is tricky. It migrates throughout the body without advance warning. One day my knees would ache. The next day my knees were fine, but the pain would have taken up residence in my elbows, neck, and feet.

Before the diagnosis, it was hard to tell exactly what was wrong. In addition to the mysterious migrating pain in my joints, I also experienced brain fog and poor sleep. Should I consult with a neurologist? An orthopedic specialist? A podiatrist? What about getting a sleep study? It seemed like my whole body was falling apart, one piece at a time. Nothing I tried seemed to help. The future was bleak. All I could see was a life hobbled by uncertain steps.

As I continued to clean up my diet in the recovery circles I attended, I also stopped eating flour, corn, white potatoes, and sugar. Lo and behold! The symptoms of fibromyalgia receded, then disappeared. Today, I'm healthier and more active than I have ever been.

It turns out that eating comfort foods like toast, popcorn, French fries, and cookies to make myself feel better in the midst of the pain didn't heal me. Just the opposite; that suite of foods prolonged and even exacerbated my symptoms. Meanwhile, I felt victimized by a disease brought on by my own doing. To heal, I had to deal with root causes.

You may think of these eight symptoms as separate problems and bring in experts from various fields to try to solve them. That may be good for a quick win. But the truth is, this suite of symptoms points to a larger problem: the lack of vision. Your congregation is not led by a Jesus-like dream. That's the common denominator underlying your ills.

Ignore this at your peril. Doing more of the same in your

ministry setting will only prolong and exacerbate your symptoms of decline. It won't fix them.

It's time now to try something brand new. It will take you out of the realm of tried and true behaviors, deep into the unknown. It won't be as predictable, but it will be exhilarating.

Now that you've identified the symptoms at play in your ministry setting, it's time to introduce you to the DARE model of dreaming like Jesus.

My **DARE** to Dream Like Jesus Plan

FIRST	SECOND	THIRD	FOURTH
DREAM like Jesus ➡	**A**LIGN Others to Your Dream ➡	**R**EALIZE the Dream ➡	**E**XPAND the Dream
1. Own Your Spiritual Authority	**1.** Identify Congregational Culture	**1.** Map Your Strategy	**1.** Count the Impacts
2. Explore the Five Surprise Elements	**2.** Create Your Rationale	**2.** Take Courageous Action	**2.** Praise Your Partnership
3. Craft Your Jesus-Like Dream	**3.** Anticipate Potential Resistance	**3.** Communicate and Celebrate	**3.** Delight in Faith

PART 2

DREAM Like Jesus

*It's time to put the DARE model into action! It all begins with **D**, for Dream. First, claim the authority that Jesus grants you to dream big. Second, uncover the five surprise elements of a Jesus-like dream. Third, create your own Jesus-like dream.*

CHAPTER FOUR

Jesus Grants You Authority to Dream Big

A few years ago, I led a "Leadership Smarts" retreat for an accomplished group of first and second career pastors. These women and men, aged twenty-seven to seventy-seven, were amply gifted and equipped for the ministries they undertook. One afternoon, as we reviewed the results of their leadership profiles, it became clear that this extraordinary group of human beings had self-concepts which were tragically small. Externally, they were doing good work. Internally, they were as hobbled by secret fears as I once was by fibromyalgia. Their fears ranged from the fear of being seen as an imposter, to making the hard decisions and getting them wrong, to not living up to their calling, to not getting things done. They also dealt with the fear of conflict and chaos, of making people mad, and the fear of being rejected. These were common fears, but why did they hound such uncommon leaders?

As I reviewed their leadership profiles, I wondered why their results weren't more consistent with their calling. It occurred to me that the problem wasn't the pastors themselves, nor the leadership profiles, nor their fears. No, the problem was theological. It was the very way they imagined themselves in relation to God. Called but incomplete, equipped but incompetent, authorized but small. It was as if they hadn't fully absorbed the very Gospel they preached.

I could relate. I thought back to my own ordination some twenty years earlier. When I was ordained as an elder in The United Methodist Church, my bishop, Mary Ann Swenson, laid her hands upon my bowed head and blessed me with the ancient phrase, "Take thou authority." While the moment was stirring, it didn't take but a year to realize I hadn't taken enough. Yes, I had authority by dint of my ordination and my position as associate pastor. But in my day-to-day dealings with people, I bumped up against circumstances, people, and situations that called out my worst instincts: people pleasing, fear of offending, and a craving to be liked. Negative thoughts and self-doubt vied for dominance with the inner authority that was beginning to take root in me. Like the pastors whose leadership profiles I was reviewing, I too often felt small, incomplete, and incompetent. Yet, those words continued to ring in my ears. *Take thou authority.*

Over the years, as I have expanded my self-concept, I have gone back to the Source for more and more authority. It's been tough – like Jacob who wrestled an angel for a blessing. To claim my authority, I have had to recover from addictions, deal with long-standing fears, resolve family of origin issues, engage a therapist, hire a coach, practice vigorous self-care, expand my own emotional intelligence, and participate in transformational leadership programs. Most of all, I've had to re-think my theology and anthropology.

I grew up with a Sunday school version of God, an Old Man in the Sky looking down on me. He, and he was definitely a he, was part policeman, part judge, part paternal influence. It took me a long time to realize it, but unconsciously my image of God bore an uncanny resemblance to Joe Scott, Jr., my father, dating back to the time he was about thirty and I was about five. My dad was a hard worker and a great provider. A big, imposing figure, he was an entrepreneur and businessman who seemed to be at the center of a complex world, one I figured I would never fully grasp. As the father of four children at the time – all born within a six-year span – he was also harried and distant. I knew he cared about all of us, but when he and my mom fought, I instinctively stayed out of the way. Cooler heads would soon prevail. But in the meantime, voices would rise, doors would slam, and the house would grow eerily quiet. I know now that I had nothing to do with the arguments, but I didn't know that then. I figured if I was a good enough girl, everything would calm down around the house. As a result, I have spent an inordinate amount of my lifespan trying to be good enough to please the "big people" in my life, most especially God.

It's normal to picture a parent writ large as God. When we are small, they are the big authorities in our lives. Even though one of the Ten Commandments instructs us to make no images of God, at some level we all try to picture God to make sense of the Divine. That's nothing new. The scriptures themselves contain many images of God. In fact, I think of the Bible as a record of humanity's evolving understanding of God.

In Genesis alone, we encounter a variety of images of God: the artistic creator of heaven and earth, the Master Gardener who joyfully plants a garden East of Eden, the tender God who places a mark of protection on Cain, and the fed up God who sends the flood in an effort to start over.[25] Later we get images of a jealous God who punishes people for idolatry or a hopeful God who sends prophets to warn people to repent. In the parables of Jesus, we get a forgiving God who welcomes back the prodigal Son from his misadventures. Not to mention God as a mother hen who watches over her chicks, and a breastfeeding mother who dandles her children on her knee. Finally, Paul gives us the image of Jesus, the Divine Incarnate, in whom the fullness of God was pleased to dwell.

The most prevalent image of God is one we barely acknowledge or know. And yet it is the most powerful one for developing internal authority. It's an image revealed to Moses out in the middle of the wilderness, in a high and dry place not unlike the high desert plains of Wyoming where I live, by an angel of the Lord. The story is told in Exodus 3-4. This angel or messenger appears to Moses, as a shrub that seems to be ablaze in fire. Moses has been out in the desert tending the flocks of his father-in-law Jethro. Suddenly, he sees a bush that is burning but somehow isn't burned up in the process. "Let me turn aside and see this thing."

When Moses gets there, God calls to him, "Moses! Moses!" He answers, "Here I am." "Do not come closer for the ground on which you are standing is holy ground. Take off your sandals." And then God introduces himself: "I am the God of your father, the God of Abraham, the God of Isaac, and the God of Jacob." The first two words of that introduction are a portent of things to come: I am.

God goes on to tell Moses that he has seen the suffering of his people who are enslaved in Egypt. "I will send you to free my People, the Israelites, from Egypt." Moses is caught off guard! "Me?" he wonders. Five times he protests: Who am I that I should do this thing? Who should I say sent me? What if they don't believe me? I can't speak. And finally, "Send somebody else."

God wins this argument and sends Moses, but not before revealing the most powerful, the most interesting, and the most overlooked name and image of God in the entire Bible. When Moses asks, Who should I say has sent me? God says, "Tell them that I AM THAT I AM" or I WILL BE WHAT I WILL BE," has sent you (Exodus 3:14).

What kind of name is this anyway? It's not a common biblical name like Joseph or Miriam. Nor is it a place name, a prophetic utterance, or a description of an historical event. These kinds of names are also common in the Bible. Rather, this is a name that describes a state of being. It's the only time this kind of name is given in the Bible. This unusual name is referred to as the Tetragrammaton, a Greek word meaning "four letters."

Yet, almost as soon as the Tetragrammaton is uttered, it's hidden from our view, covered up again. Not because this name of God isn't used again. It is, again and again, over fifty-four hundred times, in fact. Instead, the Tetragrammaton is replaced. In the English, what we see is the word LORD, all in capital letters.

Underneath these four English upper-case letters are four Hebrew letters: yod-hay-vav-hay: YHVH. Sometimes incorrectly pronounced Jehovah, YHVH comes from the Hebrew verb "to be" and can be roughly translated as "the One Who Is." For the same reason Jesus used the term Kingdom of heaven instead of Kingdom of God, the word LORD protects the holy name. This name of God is so holy that it is not even to be uttered. But not only does LORD cover up the holy name of God, it obscures a holistic understanding of God, whose name is the state of being.

The word LORD suggests a distant deity: removed, other, transcendent, not to mention awe-inspiring and even scary. But the name of God nestled underneath LORD – I AM THAT I AM – denotes a certain intimacy with an immanent Presence. (The capitalized letters are purely a function of the English language; upper and lower case distinctions do not exist in the Hebrew.) While the word LORD describes a figure or a personage, a discrete being, one who is over and above, the name I AM THAT I AM is pure verb, pure being itself. In fact, Rabbi Arthur Waskow once wrote a book called *God is a Verb*. That title is meant to capture this very idea, the "is"-ness of God; what pastor, poet, and musician Steve Garnaas-Holmes described as an "upwelling presence," and eco-theologian Sallie McFague calls "the energy empowering the entire universe."

I grew up in the hot and hazy summers of New England

where the cicadas were so loud during the day that I was never sure if the strong steady buzz I was hearing was the hum of electrical lines or those well-camouflaged insects. I knew the cicadas were out there. Yet, I could never see them. I think of God in that way. Not as a bug, of course, but as a Presence that permeates everything around us, the very essence or buzz of life.

Jesus later comes to be associated with the phrase I AM. The Gospel according to John reports Jesus saying, variously, I AM the bread of life; I AM from above; I AM the Light of the world; I AM the Son of God; I AM the resurrection and the life; I AM the way, and the truth, and the life; and I AM the true vine" (John 6:35, 8:23, 8:12, 9:5, 10:36, 11:25, 14:6, 15:1). Through the I AM sayings, Jesus shares in the being-ness of God.

If God is Being-ness itself, rather than a discrete and distant being, aka Sallie McFague's "external super person,"[26] then God is not so much the object or even subject of life, but rather the context of life. What the Apostle Paul calls "the ground of our being," and what a quantum theologian might call "the field of our being," I think of as the life essence that animates our being. If God is the context of life itself, then God is not only creator of the universe but geographically speaking, co-equal with it, found equally, everywhere.

The Psalmist, too, sensed this pervasiveness of God by affirming that there is no place where God is not.

Where shall I go from your Spirit?
  Or where shall I flee from your presence?
If I ascend to heaven, you are there!
  If I make my bed in Sheol, you are there!
If I take the wings of the morning
  and dwell in the uttermost parts of the sea,
even there your hand shall lead me,
  and your right hand shall hold me.
If I say, "Surely the darkness shall cover me,
  and the light about me be night,"
even the darkness is not dark to you;

the night is bright as the day,
for darkness is as light with you.

Psalm 139:7-12 (ESV)

You have been taught or known in some way that God is inside of you, but I would argue you have NOT realized that if God is everywhere present, not a discrete being in the sky, but the quality of Being itself, that means that each of you is inside of God, and God is inside of each of you. You are surrounded by, and suffused with, Divine Power. This idea is picked up by spiritual teacher Eric Butterworth who notes, "In the universal realm in which you live and have being, the whole of God is present at every point in space at the same time."[27]

This holistic integrated view of God, technically called panentheism,[28] or what Richard Rohr calls the "incarnational worldview,"[29] in which matter and Spirit are not artificially separated, is very different than a mechanistic view of God, in which humans are objects, being acted upon by God – or ignored by God – as the case may be.

God is already within you. You are already within God. You live in a deeply interrelated ecosystem of the Divine, of Life, of I Am-ness, where everything is interconnected and interrelated. By virtue of your inclusion in the creation, all humans are one, like cells within one giant organism. More to the point here, you are already one with Jesus and with God. It's how things are made. Consider the vine and branches imagery in John 14:20. "I am in God and God is in me and you are in us. I am in you and you are in me," Jesus says. This unity isn't in your visible form. You can't see the Divine. It's in the Beingness that permeates and interconnects all. That is the image and likeness of God, the I AM-ness that connects you with all.

Being interwoven in the I AM-ness of God grants you tremendous authority simply by virtue of your humanity. It is this state of being from which you derive your authority. It's the state of being that should vanquish all fears of not being good enough. If you are one with the Divine , how could it be any other way?

Agency

As a human being, you are created with agency. Agency is the capacity to choose what you think, decide what you believe, select how you feel, and chart the actions you take. Agency implies your inborn capacity to live a purposeful life. Interestingly, your agency is influenced by your belief as much as by your skill.

According to Jesus, owning your agency is critical. Your beliefs, in particular, are intimately connected to your ability to co-create miracles with God. Jesus was fond of pointing out, "Your faith has made you well," to those who sought healing. If your well-being, or lack thereof, unfolds according to what you believe, what else is possible?

Back when I was single, I used to take ballroom dance lessons hoping I'd meet someone on the dance floor and be swept off my feet. Before I ventured onto the dance floor, I did not understand the mechanics and art of dance. I knew the man led, but I didn't know how. What I discovered was that the graceful art of dance involved a great deal of partnership between the man and woman, or the "lead" and "follow." The man exerts very firm pressure against the woman's hand to steer the couple. But she couldn't be steered, or engage in the dance, if she doesn't exert equally firm pressure in return. This isn't a case of overpowering. If her return pressure is weak, the man simply can't lead. But if she meets his firm pressure with her own, he can steer her through intricate steps she had not even known before. While I didn't meet the man of my dreams through ballroom dance (that came later through a country two-step class) I was able to tango, foxtrot, and waltz as if I had been dancing these intricate steps all my life!

Exercising your God-given authority and agency is like ballroom dancing. As you enter into the divine dance you soon realize that it's not just about having faith in the leading partner, you also have to exercise faith in yourself. You are a critical part of the equation. The Bible makes this clear: wherever people had great faith, Jesus performed great miracles. Where they lacked faith, not much happened. Miracle-making requires equal partnership where both parties show up, equally ready, willing, and able to do their part (Matthew 13:58).

I want to let you in on a little secret: Jesus never intended to keep his wonder-working, miracle-making power to himself. Again and again, Jesus invited his disciples and apostles into this realm. Now he invites you.

Jesus wants you to dream like him, to claim authority like him, and exercise agency like him. That's why he said, "Whoever welcomes you welcomes me; and whoever welcomes me welcomes the one who sent me" (Matthew 10:40, NSRV). You are invited into the unity of God and Jesus, to be one with God, and one with Jesus. You do that by matching God's faith in you with your own faith in God, and in yourself. While you won't have the same unwavering purity of faith or depth of belief in God or yourself, that God has in you, you can rise to much greater faith.

Jesus has already shared his power, authority, miracle-making magic, passionate faith, and unity with God with you. You just didn't know it. As a result, you have been living way too small.

My own faith grew as I awakened to the stunning reality through recovery from addictions that I am a co-creator with God. Addiction creates a context of hopelessness and tells you nothing will ever change. Nothing can ever change. Yet, in partnership with this Power and Presence, my whole life has changed. God didn't wave a magic wand. It's been an evolving process of realigning my beliefs, actions, and attitudes, of claiming my agency that empowered me to recover from "a hopeless state of mind and body."[30]

You, too, co-create with God: from the smallest cells in your body to your grandest thoughts and actions. That's no small matter. As a co-creator with God, you have the power to move mountains with even just a modicum of faith. You have the power to multiply loaves and fishes, to walk on water, to cast out demons, to do everything Jesus did, and even more. Yet, how reluctant the church is to accept or reinforce the agency that Jesus affirms.

Christians have an odd relationship with power. We need it but we're not sure what to do with it. While churches teach people to run the local church, to lend a helping hands to those in need, and to participate in a variety of ministries, beyond that there is scant encouragement for people to discover their own power, to dream their own dreams, or to maximize their own potential.

A few winters ago, I was leading a "Culture Shift" retreat. A few of us were out for a walk during the break, our breaths visible in the brisk North Carolina mountain air. Henry asked me, "Why do people have such an easy time talking about Mary Kay Cosmetics and evangelizing iPhones but not talking about Jesus or inviting people to church?" It was a rhetorical question, but I had a ready answer. I had coached women who sold through direct marketing companies like Mary Kay. "I'll tell you why, Henry. Mary Kay develops women as leaders." Henry nodded. I explained that while their products are good, the business is based on how women can accomplish their dreams. "Mary Kay doesn't really promote cosmetics to their saleswomen, Henry. They promote agency, and then train them how to use that agency." Even as my breath crystallized in the now freezing air, I warmed up to my subject. Same thing with iPhones, I explained. The TV commercials are not about iPhones. They are about freedom and self-expression, the ability to fully live your life. If you have an iPhone, you have power and freedom to express yourself any way you want. The phone isn't about phone calls.

It's about pictures, and connections, and videos. Mary Kay gets it. Apple gets it. But the church doesn't. "In the church, Henry, we don't talk about what's in it for members."

In church, the focus is on doing for others. That's good, as far as that goes. But do you focus on your own self, on how God dwells within you, and what that means for your self-development? You miss something critical when you gloss over yourself. You, too, have personal power and potential. And so do the people you serve.

Are you afraid that your individual agency takes away from that of Jesus? It doesn't. Yes, you need God. But diminishing yourself in the process decreases God's ability to co-create miracles with you. Owning your agency releases the divine power within you.

After all, Jesus was all about empowering his disciples. He showed them how to tap into increasing power, agency, ability, and capacity. Then, he entrusted his entire ministry to them. The power they tapped into was God-given. That's the power you are invited to tap into as well for the good of all.

Remember the "Leadership Smarts" retreat I told you about at the beginning of the chapter? Interestingly, one young pastor had a large and sprawling graph. It was a self-concept more in touch with his call and his visions than his experience in the church. "Should I not think so highly of myself?" he asked the group. "Should I come down to earth?" Before I could formulate an answer, one of his colleagues piped up, "No! Keep your dreams alive."

Now that you've been reminded that Jesus grants you authority and invites you to exercise your agency, and you've considered unity with God from a new perspective, let's take a look at the five surprise elements to a Jesus-like dream.

DREAM like Jesus

Own Your Spiritual Authority	
Go to mydreamlikejesus.com. Download the set of worksheets so that you can apply what you are learning. Alone or with a team, write out the following:	**Own Your Spiritual Authority** ▪ _____ ▪ _____ ▪ _____ ▪ _____ ▪ _____

- **Your unique calling**
  Identify the key elements of your unique calling. How did you get to where you are?

- **Your distinctive credentials**
  List the life experiences, trainings, and education that make you who you are.

- **Miracles you've already made with God**
  Recount the surprising events-both small and large-you and God have collaborated on to date.

- **Fears you've overcome**
  Name the fears that have released their grip on you in part or in whole.

- **Declare your spiritual authority**
  Claim and give thanks for your spiritual authority.

CHAPTER FIVE

Five Surprise Elements
of a Jesus-Like Dream

A Jesus-like dream has five surprising elements. First, it expands assumptions about what is possible. It's feisty, it's spirited, it's big, and it's bold. A Jesus-like dream doesn't rubber stamp what is already in place. Nor does it kowtow to current circumstances. It doesn't give in and it doesn't give up. It doesn't say I can't. It says with God, we can. It doesn't conform to self-imposed limitations. Rather, brand new realities arise from this kind of vision.

Second, a Jesus-like dream is bigger than you are. It's not something you can do all by yourself. You can't provide jobs and housing for all the homeless, you can't inspire meaning in the lives of all teenage boys, and you certainly can't eradicate racism on your own. It will take a community of invigorated dreamers to realize those big dreams. Frankly, even you and your community aren't big enough to realize truly big dreams. Fulfilling big dreams goes beyond mere human power. You will need an infusion of divine guidance and power. In other words, you need God. That's the nature of a Jesus-like dream.

Third, a Jesus-like dream scares you. Just how will you tackle the opioid epidemic in your community? Or how will you ensure that all children fulfill their God-given potential? These aspirations sound great on paper – and they may give you warm fuzzies – but conceiving such lofty dreams also evokes a measure of fear. It has to. Why? Because if you're perfectly comfortable with a vision, then either you're not paying attention to the size of the endeavor or your dream is not big enough. If there's no fear factor, the dream you're entertaining doesn't require God's help and guidance. A Jesus-like dream has a mystique, a whiff of the mysterious. It excites, even as it defies doing. And it terrifies even as it calls to you. You'd be surprised how scary love can be.

Fourth, a Jesus-like dream is about the flourishing of the community, not merely the survival of an institution. Notice Jesus didn't pray, "Thy Kingdom come, thy will be done in First Synagogue of Nazareth." A Jesus-like dream is bigger than any one worshiping congregation. It's more expansive than a single group of people. It's about all of us, not just some of us. It's about the New Reign and Realm of God, the Beloved Community.

If you've tried visions intended to grow your worship service or re-invigorate your Sunday school, you know these types of visions don't create a sustainable culture shift, because they are too inward-focused. They also don't engage enough new people to create fresh energy or generate much forward momentum. You and the same twenty percent who do everything else are left exhausted.

A Jesus-like dream approaches things differently. Instead of the congregation being the focus of the vision, in a Jesus-like dream, the church and its people are the agent of the vision. The focus is your neighborhood, your community, your region, or your world. "How can we do that, you ask, if we can't even grow our worship service or Sunday school?" As you develop a Kingdom-oriented vision, your church will feel compelled to operate at a higher level of effectiveness, increasing its giving, and expanding its prayer life.

In my work with United Methodists, I challenge the keepers of the vision – whether they be the chief missional strategists, the vision midwives, or the boots on the ground

– to focus on their denominational mission, "To make disciples of Jesus Christ for the transformation of the world." In
church-speak, making disciples often devolves into attempts
to increase worship attendance or bolster Sunday school
numbers. I invite people, instead, to focus on the second half
of the mission statement: for the transformation of the world.
As you envision how to make a real difference in the world,
you begin to truly follow Jesus.

Fifth, a Jesus-like dream inspires and unifies people. Like
a campfire draws people to its warmth on a chilly night,
a shared vision of a positive future draws people together
as well. Such an inviting vision promises a reassuring
future which bolsters well-being and addresses the needs of
the community and Creation. It supplies something that's
missing, elevates the way things are done, or meets a longing
in an unprecedented fashion. A Jesus-like dream pledges an
experience of relatedness in which people feel one with God,
one with each other, and one with all Creation. It generates a
sense of unity, of indivisibility; all for one and one for all.

Even as a radiant vision draws people in, the truth is, not
everyone is going to be happy about it. Adopting a Jesus-sized
dream isn't for everyone. Sometimes people aren't up for
big, bold, feisty, or spirited visions. That's okay. Let them be.
Jesus did.

Are you ready to dream like Jesus? Great! Before you push
off into deeper waters, though, there's one more thing to
keep in mind. You've got to be willing to ask too much. "The
problem with passion," Richard Rohr writes in *Radical Grace,*
"isn't that we desire too much, in spite of what moralists used
to tell us. The real problem is that we don't desire enough."[31]
Even if they don't know it, the world wants more of churches:
more spirituality, more community, more engagement, more
love, more miracles, more demonstration of the Kingdom.

Yet most of you attend, serve, or supervise shrinking,
declining, dying churches. If your leadership is to be effec-

tive, if you are about manifesting the Kingdom here on earth, if you are to make a true difference in the lives of those you lead and the communities you serve, you need to dream even bigger. Think about it. If the vision isn't bigger than you are, then you won't need God's power and presence to fulfill it. If it doesn't require God's touch, it won't be worthy of the church. Your dream has to be worth it. Otherwise, you'll lose interest, and frankly, so will everyone else.

Friends, it's time to stop playing small. It's time to stop feeling constrained by circumstances or limited by what's happened in the past. Circumstances and limitations never stopped Jesus. And they needn't stop you.

As you begin to dream like Jesus, let the prayer of sixteenth century sea explorer Sir Francis Drake guide you.

Disturb us Lord when we are too well pleased with ourselves, when our dreams have come true because we have dreamed too little, when we arrived safely because we sailed too close to the shore. . .. Disturb us Lord, to dare more boldly, to venture on wilder seas where storms will show Your mastery; where losing sight of land, we shall find the stars. We ask you to push back the horizons of our hopes, and to push back the future in strength, courage, hope, and love.

I, myself, am so inspired by Jesus' big dreams and the authority he grants that I have created my own Jesus-like dream to guide my work, my decisions, and my choices. Here it is: I'm committed to empower the worldwide body of Christ to take a quantum leap of faith into dreaming like Jesus. When this vision is fulfilled, we'll see Jesus' friends, fans, and followers manifesting miracles that create a world that works for everyone, with no one and nothing left out.

Let's test this vision against the five surprise elements of a Jesus-like dream. First, my vision of the Kingdom certainly expands assumptions about what's possible. Right now, the common wisdom is that the church is on its way out, gasping its last breath. We can't do more than we are doing. Second, my dream is way bigger than I am. There's no way I can achieve this vision by myself. Third, it scares me. Simply thinking about how visible I have to be, how many risks I have to take, how much cooperation I need is enough to stall me sometimes. Am I afraid? You bet! How the heck could I possibly pull this off?

I don't have the tools, strategies, and resources to do it on my own. Fourth, this vision is outward-focused. It's not about my survival. Rather it's about the world-wide body of Christ, including people I will never know or meet. Fifth, my vision has inspired other people to dream big. It frees up other spiritual leaders to imagine their future and the future of the church in a brand-new way. I can hear the excitement in their voices. I've also witnessed how my big vision attracts the support of others. One colleague was so moved by it that she approached me about applying for a $1 million grant to expand this work across the country. She even offered to write the grant! Clearly, this vision of the world-wide body of Christ dreaming like Jesus taps into people's positive hopes for the future.

Your vision can do the same. Now that you've considered unity with God from a new perspective, and you've learned the five surprise elements of a Jesus-like dream, and you've peeked at my own Jesus-like dream are you ready to try this for yourself? In the following chapter, I will show you how.

DREAM like Jesus

Explore the Five Surprise Elements	

Go to mydreamlikejesus.com.
Download or continue completing the worksheets.

Alone or with a team, write out the following:

- **Assumptions**
  Identify assumptions that limit what you think is possible for yourself, your congregation, and your community.

- **Bigger Than You Are**
  Brainstorm what could be possible if you didn't have to do everything by yourself.

- **It Scares You**
  If you knew you could not fail, what might you try?

- **The Kingdom, Not the Congregation**
  Generate ideas about what your community needs from you.

- **Inspire and Unify**
  What aspirational outcomes would get your people energized and bring them together?

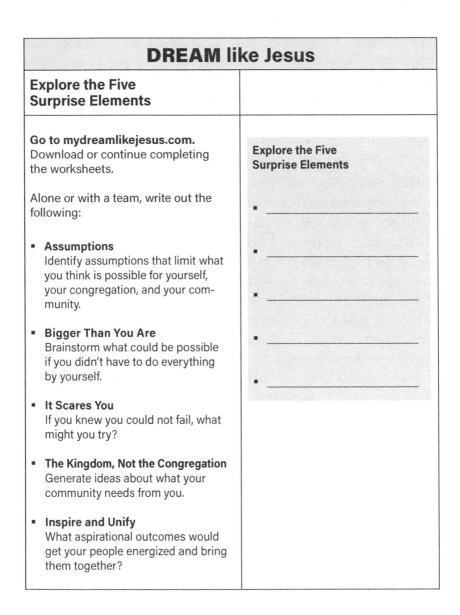

Explore the Five Surprise Elements

- _____

- _____

- _____

- _____

- _____

CHAPTER SIX

How to Create Your Own Jesus-Like Dream

As a Christian leader, you, have the dreams of God planted within you. Your task of leadership, your greatest act of stewardship, is to dare to bring forth that dream, then to lead people in its realization. As you consider what dreams these might be, taste these pungent words from *Radical Grace* by Richard Rohr.

> *What word of hope does the church have to offer the world? The world is tired of our ideas and ideologies. It's tired of our lazy church services. It's no longer going to believe ideas, but it will believe love. It will believe life that is given and received... For most people in the world the question is not, Is there life on the other side of death? It is, rather, Is there life on this side of death?*[32]

A Jesus-like dream enables people to experience the glory of being alive while on earth.

As you dare to create your own Jesus-like dream, let's take a moment and distinguish some key terms, starting with mission and vision. Your congregation's mission is the reason it exists. Your vision is the imagined aspirational future your congregation is living into. To borrow from the leadership wisdom of Glenn Howell, vision is how you ideally see yourself doing your mission

To get a clear picture of the difference, let's look at a specific example. In The United Methodist Church, "Making disciples of Jesus Christ for the transformation of the world" is the current denominational mission. It's the reason that the church exists at this time. Based on what I've observed, the working vision of the denomination is, "A world in which the hungry are fed, diseases are stamped out, and God's grace is made known to all." Most United Methodist Churches I've worked with have some sort of food ministry. The denomination champions an international campaign that invites people to "Imagine No Malaria." Finally, United Methodists are big on extending the grace of God.

Notice that when it comes to the United Methodist's working vision, not every detail is nailed down, nor is every nuance figured out. "A world in which the hungry are fed, diseases are stamped out, and God's grace is made known to all," paints a picture of the future with broad brush strokes. It's more like an artistic rendering of a faraway mountain rather than a close-up photo of an immediate landscape.

Now let's distinguish between a vision and a goal. While a vision is by definition way bigger than you, a goal is smaller, more defined, and can easily have the details for its implementation supplied. Goals are necessary to enact a vision. But they are not the vision itself.

For instance, one goal necessary to carry out the United Methodist vision might be, "Hold weekly worship services in every congregation so that people in the community can hear and learn about the love of God." While weekly worship services are a good thing, they are one goal that moves you toward the vision, but they are not the vision. How do you know? Implementing this goal won't necessarily lead to a world in which the hungry are fed, diseases are stamped out, and the grace of God is made known to all.

Let's tell the truth. It's easier to settle for a goal than it is to reach for a dream. It's easier to take on something small, do-able, and predictable than it is to risk something that might fail. You might even be tempted to do so. But you've picked up this book. Something in you yearns for something more than same old, same old. I encourage you to resist the temptation to settle for a goal and go all the way for a Jesus-like dream.

Let's say you have had a dream for your church. You can see what would make for a really great, healthy, functioning church: more folks in worship, more outreach ministries, more Bible study, more youth, and above all, more help! Let's say your vision is this: "Community Church of the Awesome will be a vibrant church that reaches out to people of all ages with excellent worship, intimate small groups, and effective outreach that touches lives." That's a nice picture, isn't it? Yes, as far as it goes. An active congregation like this might even be an engaging church to attend.

As a Jesus-like dream, though, this vision doesn't go far enough. Jesus didn't come to make Judaism great again. And he didn't live and die simply for your church to grow. Rather, his purpose was greater still. He came to give birth to a dream, the biggest dream a person could imagine: that all of heaven would be reflected here on earth. "Thy Kingdom come, thy will be done, on earth as it is in heaven." Your vision needs to rise to that level of audacity, chutzpah if you will, to have a Kingdom impact. How do you get there?

Here's the key piece. Lift your gaze from the ideal of growing a really great church to what a really great church could contribute to the Kingdom itself. For instance, let's say Community Church of the Awesome actually transforms itself into a vibrant church which reaches out to people of all ages with excellent worship, intimate small groups, and effective outreach that touches lives. Let's say that's a reality. Are you with me? Now, what would your community be like if your church actually functioned in that way? How would your community be different if the awesome people of Community Church functioned the way you suspect they could? If they really believed that God is within them, that Jesus has empowered them, that they could do greater things than even Jesus did, what sort of larger impact would they have on the neighborhood, the city, the country, the world? What might they take on that would ripple out into the community you are there to serve?

Is that hard for you to imagine? I'm often surprised how hard it is for faithful, even visionary, spiritual leaders to imagine the impact their church can have on their community. Maybe that's why our impact is limited. As Jesus points out, you have to believe it to see it.

Take the case of Rev. Steve Trout, a friendly, fun-loving pastor who enjoyed a satisfying forty-year stint in the ministry, with all the attendant highs and lows one might expect over four decades of working with people. Until recently, he pastored in a unique community in which Main Street sports a sixty-inch plexiglass screen featuring the movements of the Mars Rover. The Mars Rover was developed out of the Los Alamos National Laboratories, a government research facility based there focused on developing nuclear energy, nuclear medicine, and nuclear weapons.

When we first met, Steve was about six years out from retirement. He wanted to end his active ministry on a high note and not just mark time until his pension checks began to arrive. Like most pastors, he wanted his church to have excellent worship, functioning ministries, and a growing congregation. Steve was thinking along those lines when he joined one of my *Creating a Culture of Renewal*® groups. He started exploring visions that captured those ideals. Every time he came to me with one such vision, I challenged him. "Steve, is that big enough?" He began to reconsider what his congregation was actually capable of as I pushed him to expand his assumptions about what was possible. He went from a church focus to a community focus to a Kingdom focus. Here's what I mean. His first vision was "Connect disciples with Jesus Christ, grow disciples to maturity in Jesus Christ, care for disciples in Christian fellowship, and send disciples into mission and ministry." I pushed him.

"What would happen if these goals were met, really fulfilled? What would we see your church actually doing? How would your community be different?" He went silent, his head tipped to the side, his normally sunny face screwed into a thoughtful scowl as he contemplated the question. "Lemme think about that."

I push people to expand their assumptions and lift their gaze because it's what Jesus did. Remember he took twelve regular, every day people and empowered them with his very own mega vision and agency so that they could perform miracles. Do you think that when little Andrew and Simon were growing up, they aspired to be traveling, miracle-making apostles? I doubt that was on their radar screen. They knew they were headed out to the wind-swept Sea of Galilee like their father, grandfather, and great-grandfather before them to make a living. They would spend their lives fixing and casting nets, finding plentiful spots to fish, and hauling in the catch of the day. They never could have predicted that they would move from catching fish to catching people's imagination with Jesus' big dream. But Jesus dared them with a larger vision and purpose. "I'll make a new kind of fisherman out of you. I'll show you how to catch men and women instead of perch and bass" (Matthew 4:19 MSG). When they accepted his offer, they traded out their limited perspectives of their future for something they couldn't have imagined.

As a visionary leader, that's your job, too. People assume that at their best, churches provide a place to get centered, to connect with friends, to pray and sing, get grounded in the Bible, and maybe even hear from God. They don't really think it's possible for them to do the very things that Jesus did and more. Yet, the scriptures promise, "Very truly, I tell you, the one who believes in me will also do the works that I do and, in fact, will do greater works than these, because I am going to the Father" (John 14:12, NIV). So, spiritual leader, expanding your assumptions about what is possible is a necessary act of faith. Get big, get bold, get outrageous! That's the Christ-like, biblical way of doing things.

Steve began to think about the real impact his congregation could have on his community if they already had excellent worship, functioning ministries, and a growing congregation. He came back to me with what I call a community vision: "People in our community could be inspired to live better lives." "That's a good start, Steve," I countered, "but what kind of better life? What would that actually look like?" I wanted Steve to move from a generalized community-oriented vision to a more specific and inspiring Kingdom-oriented vision that he and his people could actually wrap their heads around and bring to life.

Steve went away to think some more. As he did, a new dream began to take shape deep within him. Although he pastored in the richest community in the whole state of New Mexico, hidden pockets of poverty were tucked into trailer parks and cloaked behind week-to-week wages. This is the state of affairs in a county with one of the highest median incomes in the US.[33] What if his church could address the people impacted by low wages? Half a dozen other agencies and outreach programs were already ministering to the hungry in his community. But Steve realized there were still people falling through the cracks. He had ministered to more than one mother who wasn't sure how to make ends meet. Elementary school teachers attended church and lifted up the children who came to school hungry, with little appetite for learning or behaving. How could parents do well at their job if they were worried about their kids? How could students learn if their growling stomachs demanded more attention than the lessons of the day?

The more Steve thought about this, the more what had previously seemed impossible now became an imperative. He came back to me with his answer. "This church could end hunger in our community!" "Now that's a Kingdom vision," I responded.

"A Hunger to End Hunger!" became his rallying cry. "Our congregation could spearhead efforts to make sure no one in our community ever goes hungry again," he told me. After all, Steve pointed out, it was the apostles themselves who multiplied a few fish and loaves of bread. Jesus blessed this meager offering, yes, but it wasn't until the food passed through the apostles' hands that the multiplication began.

Now you may ask, "Does the church really need to do this kind of work?" After all, what makes feeding the hungry different from what community or government agencies do? Leave food to them and worship to the church, you might think. But, remember Jesus' big dream: "Thy Kingdom come, thy will be done, on earth as it is heaven." Jesus envisioned an earth that reflected the unconditional love, light, joy, beauty, and magnificence of a world in which God's Presence would be unmistakable, where the Kingdom would be fully present. Steve could lead his church to meet a prerequisite of it. He realized that Jesus fed people who were hungry so that they could hear his teaching. He did it as an act of love. Steve figured the bottom line is God's love. When people know that God loves them unconditionally and unequivocally, they can be empowered to do and become anything they desire. Love, connected with food, would be the gift of the church to the community. In this way, they would manifest the Kingdom around them.

Arriving at the vision is a process and a journey, one that requires exploration. That means giving yourself time to think new thoughts and explore new ideas. It means cultivating the willingness to see things from a new perspective. For spiritual leaders, this will likely involve prayer, meditation, scripture reading, and consulting other spiritual resources. Remember, the vision will be bigger than you are. You will need God's help for the finances, the resources, the people-power. And when it is complete, the vision will serve more than your church or congregation. It will advance the loving purposes of God and manifest the Kingdom in some way. So, it makes sense that it will take some time and exploration to visualize a dream that is worthy of pursuing.

Spend some time in prayer and meditation exploring the dreams God may be bringing to your awareness. Discover the margins of your thinking, of your experience, of your logic, of your resources, and of what you think is possible. Then, consider the words of preacher Frederick Beuchner, "The place God calls you to is the place where your deep gladness and the world's deep hunger meet."[34] Ask yourself what brings you deep gladness? How about your congregation? What brings them deep gladness? What are some of the world's deep hungers? Finally, what resources does your congregation or group have that can be shared?

The intersection of these things may point to a vision. What do you see in that intersection?

Again, resist the temptation to settle for the small and predictable. Otherwise, you will miss out on the thrill of co-creating miracles with God.

The process of visioning isn't as mysterious as it might seem. The answers are within and around you. It may simply be a matter of paying attention. In fact, the more you pay attention to this process, the more visions may come to mind. If you're naturally visionary, you may feel overwhelmed by the amount of ideas that surface. Not to worry. As Maxie Dunham famously wrote, "Not every need is a call." If you're not naturally visionary, you may feel excited and energized. Alternatively, you may worry that you can't muster a vision. If so, practice cultivating a sense of curiosity. Look for the needs or problems that have your name on them. Then scale up your answers and solutions until you move from mere problem-solving to a positive picture of a God-shaped future. Trust God to partner with you. Trust yourself as you tap into an unceasing flow of creative energies.

I believe that this world is evolving toward the fulfillment of Jesus' dream. But we often get stuck in small-minded

72

eddies, unable to flow freely toward the vision. I believe the purpose of spiritual leadership is to chart a course toward the fulfillment of the Divine dream, God's Kingdom here on earth as it is in heaven.

My Jewish background and grounding in Hebrew Bible prophets has shaped my vision of the Kingdom. I envision this Kingdom to be a state in which all the world is at peace, all people prosper, and we live in harmony with each other, the Earth, and her ecosystems. In other words, we know ourselves to be one with God, one with each other, and one with the Creation itself. It all starts with being at peace with ourselves, being one with ourselves, the Kingdom of heaven, and the Divine presence that dwells within. When you truly know and sense this, you tap into an inestimable co-creative power within you.

DREAM like Jesus

Craft Your Jesus-Like Dream	

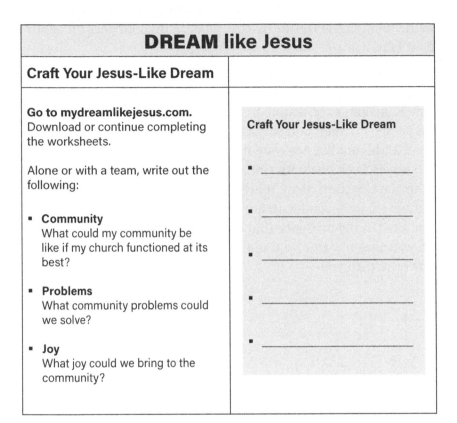

Go to **mydreamlikejesus.com.**
Download or continue completing the worksheets.

Alone or with a team, write out the following:

- **Community**
  What could my community be like if my church functioned at its best?

- **Problems**
  What community problems could we solve?

- **Joy**
  What joy could we bring to the community?

Craft Your Jesus-Like Dream

- _____

- _____

- _____

- _____

- _____

PART 3

ALIGN Others to Your Dream

*In the second step of the DARE model, **A** is for Align. Learn the art and importance of aligning others to your dream. First, get people on board with your dream. Second, provide solid reasons and rationale. Third, be prepared to engage the positive power of pushback.*

CHAPTER SEVEN

Get People on Board

Years ago, I lived in Denver where the Rocky Mountains rise abruptly from the plains of the Mile High City. I loved the quick drive up I-70 into the mountains to hike and ski. The highway winds steeply through the foothills into the pitched mountains. It's so steep that going back down, the highway is punctuated with long gravel pull-outs as a safeguard for trucks that lose their brakes. Lulled into a relaxed posture after a day in the mountains, I saw yellow caution signs that grabbed my attention: "Truckers, you are not down yet." The warnings noted the grade of the road and the miles still to go until the highway leveled out.

I'm reminded of those signs now because once you've dared to dream like Jesus, it's easy to think that you're in the clear, past all dangers and obstacles. But I have a similar warning for you: "Leader, you're not done leading yet!" Having a vision is great. But it's just the first step in dreaming like Jesus. What comes next is even more important. You will need to invite others to align with your dream. Without that support, your vision will go nowhere. Alignment is the difference between a Jesus-like dream or vision and wishful thinking. In *The Work of Leaders: How Vision, Alignment, and Execution Will Change the Way You Lead,* authors Julie Straw, Mark Scullard, Susie Kukkonen, and Barry Davis argue that ". . . leaders have three fundamental responsibilities: They craft a *vision,* they build *alignment,* and they champion *execution.*"[35] The process they outline and the best practices they highlight have greatly informed my thinking about how to bring a Jesus-like dream to fruition. In particular, when it comes to alignment, they note the importance of instilling "passion, commitment, understanding, and motivation in others."[36]

Alignment, also called buy-in, accomplishes two things. First, it increases the number of people who are aware of and committed to your Jesus-like dream. Second, it increases the ability of the vision to be realized, and for its impact to be expanded. More on that later. For now, know this. More visions falter for lack of buy-in than any other reason. Without buy-in, one of two things happen. The vision either succeeds or it fails. If you're lucky, the vision fails. If you're not so lucky, the vision moves forward, but you bear the burden of implementing it yourself. Without alignment, all the work will fall back on your shoulders, Unable to fully accomplish it on your own, either your vision will get buried, or you will.

Unlike some spiritual leaders today, Jesus wasn't trying to do all the work himself. In fact, he knew that if the message ended with him, it would die when he did. He intentionally gained buy-in from others. Then, he used their buy-in to realize his Kingdom dream.

When Jesus began announcing the Kingdom of heaven was at hand, he didn't just leave it at that. Instead, he embarked on gaining alignment. He started at his childhood synagogue in Nazareth by proclaiming that Isaiah's prophetic words had been fulfilled in their hearing. "The Spirit of the Lord is on me, because he has anointed me to preach good news to the poor, he has sent me to proclaim freedom for the prisoners and recovery of sight for the blind, and to release the oppressed, to proclaim the year of the Lord's favor" (Luke 4:18-19, NIV).

Jesus wanted and needed their buy-in. Indeed, his fellow Jews spoke well of him. But when Jesus began to goad them, their approval turned to anger. In the end, Jesus was right. He was not accepted as a prophet in his own hometown (Luke 4:20-29). The moral of the story? You don't need buy-in from everyone to make your vision a reality. But you do need a critical mass of support.

On the one hand, you may balk at the idea of not having everyone on board, fearing that it will cause disruption, that people won't be happy, or that you'll lose membership. Honestly, you might. The other option, though, is that no bold vision is lifted up, no forward movement is sought, and the church declines anyway. You may go down at peace with each other, but you will go down. Risk is involved, no doubt about it.

On the other hand, you may be glad to hear that consensus is not needed. But hold your horses! This doesn't mean that you can skip alignment altogether. You'll still need vigorous buy-in.

Let's look at how Jesus gained alignment. First, he called disciples, then he appointed them as apostles, and finally he taught them intensively about his vision. Some of these folks had previously been disciples of John the Baptist. Others were fellow Galileans such as Andrew, Peter, James, and John. While the Gospels boast differing lists of "The Twelve," and we don't know their exact identities, there's no doubt Jesus had a tight inner circle of people who supported him and bought into his vision. Even when other disciples walked away, the twelve remained steadfast (John 6:66-69).

That's not to say that the disciples always understood the vision, at least not at first. Jesus spent three intense years replicating his passion, commitment, understanding, and motivation in them. Even after all of that, Judas missed the point (John 13:21-26). Getting people's buy-in wasn't just a one-time process, nor did Jesus appeal only to the twelve. When he had buy-in at one place, he went on to the next. Then, he started the three-step process all over again: proclaiming his dream, aligning others to it, and empowering them to bring it into reality.

Understand Congregational Culture

To be effective at getting others on board with your dream, you need to have a working knowledge of the way your people operate. What are they passionate about? What are they committed to? What motivates them? In other words, you need to know your culture.

Jesus had an innate understanding of Judaism and its cultures since he was Jewish. But more than that, he understood the natural human variations in pace, preference, perspectives, and sense of power he encountered along the way. He innately grasped the expectations, fears, and motivators of the different groups he interacted with on his journeys. For instance, he treated Martha, Mary, and Lazarus differently than Simon and Andrew, and the disciples differently than the crowds who followed him. Much of this nuance we attribute to Jesus' divinity. However, in their 2015 book, *The Emotional Intelligence of Jesus: Relational Smarts for Religious Leaders,* Roy M. Oswald and Arland Jacobson [37] point out that Jesus' skill in discernment is less about his divinity than his well-developed emotional intelligence. That's good news for us. It means Jesus' relational skills are duplicable by us.

When it comes to getting your people on board with your Jesus-like dream, you'll need to develop relational smarts

or emotional intelligence as well. As you do, one key place
to apply it is in understanding the culture of your congregation. Culture is the way a group does things. So knowing the
culture of a congregation will give you lots of clues about how
to go about inviting others into the dream so you can build
and retain broad-based support.

Let's take a closer look at congregational culture and its
influence. The culture of a particular congregation impacts
how the group worships, celebrates, mourns, prays, handles
money, does ministry, approaches justice, welcomes newcomers, deals with conflict, treats its leaders, educates its people,
interacts with the community, relates to God, experiences
Jesus, and connects to the Spirit. On an intuitive level, you
can often sense the group's culture from the moment you
walk in the door. Or, you can gather information about it
from observing the way they function. (By the way, it's not
just congregations that have a culture. All groups do. So, this
information also applies to committees as well as regions,
districts, and even entire denominations.)

To get a clearer picture of your church's culture, I like to use
the following four archetypes, followed by an example of this
kind of church culture in action.[38]

Get 'er Done Culture. In groups like this, everyone stays
busy. The congregation is more focused on results than relationships. Do it yourself-ers outnumber collaborators, so
collaborative teams are less common forms of ministry in this
kind of congregation. Instead, individuals will simply take
matters into their own hands. In the Get 'er Done Culture,
a sense of urgency prevails. Yet, while everyone is busy, not
everyone is going in the same direction. When a group like
this doesn't have a strong leader to guide them, church life can
feel disconnected and chaotic. However, when groups like this
unite under their leadership – both clergy and laity – there's a
sense of purpose and forward motion.

St. Urban of the City has a Get 'Er Done Culture. It's a bold and dynamic congregation. They lead the way when it comes to embracing change, taking bold stances on controversial issues, and adopting different worship styles. The priest is forthright and outspoken. You know where this congregation stands on issues. Personal spiritual growth, however, may not be emphasized. God is experienced as directive and emboldening, who challenges and dares on behalf of a higher purpose. Discipleship is a demanding, action-oriented process that calls forth courage, adventure, and a certain amount of independence. Church is a setting for independent thinkers who take bold action on behalf of the Kingdom of God. Faith is demonstrated through decisive action.

Get 'er Done with Fun Culture. Groups like this are people-oriented. They are also fun, energetic, high-spirited, and action-oriented. In groups like this, relationships matter. New people are welcomed and integrated easily into the life of the church. Feelings are freely expressed, leading to a sense of warm connection. If relationships sour, however, a dark cloud can hang over the group. Gossip can become dominant as people struggle with feeling left out.

Happy Church is an example of a Get 'er Done with Fun congregation in action. It's a high energy, friendly, and optimistic congregation. You get a hug and a smile every time you walk in the door. In this upbeat, positive place, everyone always seems happy. You get a feeling of belonging to this fun church, even if you're not exactly sure what they stand for! God is portrayed as positive, innovative, surprising, and unpredictable. Discipleship requires positive optimism, an upbeat attitude, trust, and is built around feelings as much as actions. The church is an exciting and inclusive force for good in the world. Faith is demonstrated through saying yes.

Get er' Done by Consensus Culture. Groups like this specialize in taking care of people and tending relationships over time. These groups tend to be more low-key than the first two. Harmony and stability, more than energy or urgency, are the values that shape congregations like this. A desire for consensus, rather than independence, is a hallmark of this culture. A high value is placed on tradition and continuity. When a group like this faces conflict or high levels of uncertainty, it can grind to a halt. When things are going well, it may feel like First Church of the Stable.

First Church of the Stable has a Get 'Er Done by Consensus Culture. This congregation values tradition over innovation, minimizes conflict at all costs, and would rather their style of worship remain consistent and predictable. Every year the homecoming committee honors thirty, forty, and fifty-year members with a certificate and special words of thanks and blessing. Regular pastoral visits are expected in this congregation. God is experienced as comforting, supportive, loyal, patient, and stabilizing. Discipleship depends on the qualities of teamwork, cooperation, stability, and loyalty. Church itself is portrayed as a relaxed group of friendly people who unhurriedly focuses on the common good. Faith is demonstrated through reliability.

Get 'er Done Right Culture. Congregations like this place a high value on rational thinking and logical processes. Outwardly, people are not terribly expressive, although they feel deeply within. When it comes to decision-making, relationships generally take a back seat to facts and figures. Under pressure, perfectionism pervades, interpersonal communication lessens, and ministries stall out as analysis paralysis sets in.

When things are going well, St. Abacus is an example of this culture in action. A low-key congregation, St. Abacus has conscientiously taken on a few mission projects in the neighborhood. They want to do the right thing, but it takes them a long time to decide what that might be. Because they carefully weigh pros and cons, and pay close attention to the budget, it's sometimes hard for them to move forward. God is portrayed as reliable and deliberate with exacting, high standards, whom it is important to correctly understand and follow. Discipleship requires a calculated risk as well as spiritual and emotional maturity. The church sees itself as a thoughtful organization which carefully analyzes and does the correct thing. Faith equals understanding.

As you can see, churches get things done in a variety of ways. It all depends on the culture. The focus may be on results, action-oriented relationships, stability or accuracy. But it's not always that cut and dried. While one of these four vignettes may well describe your church, it's more likely that you have a combination culture which exhibits qualities from two or more archetypes. Most mainline churches these days, regardless of denomination, tilt toward the Get 'er Done by Consensus and Get 'er Done Right Cultures. Because churches like First Church of the Stable and St. Abacus are somewhat risk-averse, and slower to take action, they often miss opportunities to respond to changing situations. When they do take action, maintaining stable relationships and developing reliable processes is a key motivator. That means they are unlikely to try things that could fail or that would interrupt the status quo. You can see both the brilliance of this approach and the liability. On the up-side, they are likely to maintain important relationships and keep everyone happy. On the down-side, they are unlikely to want to take on a dream that scares them, or to risk too much social capital or financial outlay.

Yet, Jesus calls you to dream big. How do you do that if you have a Get 'Er Done by Consensus or Get 'Er Done Right culture? Understanding your group culture is key. It determines how you effectively share your vision as well as how to gain buy-in. It also impacts what sort of push-back you'll get as you work to realize your dream.

In fact, now that you've dreamed up a new, positive, inspiring future that dignifies and builds others up, and manifests the Kingdom in your midst – whether you have worked with a vision team to arrive at this point or woke up with it intact one morning – this is the time to cultivate alliances that bring the impossible to life. To ensure the fulfillment of your dream, you'll want to make sure that your people can really take ownership of it. That means you've got to get a deeper handle on the group culture you're operating in.

Look back over the four congregational culture archetypes. Which ones best represent your congregation? While there are nuances in every culture, and every person within a congregation, look at the broad brushstrokes to give you an entry point for action. If you're not sure how to determine your group culture, visit my website at **www.rebekahsimon-peter.com** to take the free Group Culture assessment.

As you begin to pinpoint your group culture, the next question is how to communicate your message in a way that will motivate their passion and commitment. If you've got aspects of a **Get 'er Done Culture**, be direct as you focus on the kind of results that come when you dare to rise to a big challenge. Let them know your Jesus-like dream requires adventure and risk, and that it promises results that will make a tangible difference in your community. These Christians respond well to big, bold, direct requests that require decisive action. They also respond well to challenging, competitive situations. If the stakes are high enough, they willingly lead such efforts.

If your church likes to **Get 'er Done with Fun**, then be energetic and expressive in your communication. Focus your messaging on the idea that your Jesus-like dream creates something new, positive, and innovative that meets future needs, contributes to the community, and places value on connecting people. These Christians respond well to enthusiastic appeals that generate excitement. Involve them in your efforts by asking them to make personal contacts, to plan celebrations, and to breathe new life into faltering efforts.

If your congregation has a **Get 'er Done by Consensus Culture**, then emphasize how your dream creates sustainability. Let them know that your vision ensures an enduring presence, that it creates stability in the face of uncertainty, and calm in the midst of the storm. Because these folks value loyalty to previous generations and continuity with succeeding generations, they'll appreciate the safety of stability. These Christians work well behind the scenes to support such efforts

If your congregation has a **Get 'er Done Right Culture**, then highlight character and intentionality in your messaging. They need to know that the vision has worth and value, that it meets high standards, and helps them fulfill a Christian duty by doing things correctly. Get 'er Done Christians appreciate dreams that express spiritual maturity and are grounded in logical processes. They respond well to facts, figures, and statistics. These well-organized details support their decision-making process and help them act from their highest character. They make and respond well to logical appeals.

The truth is that incorporating aspects of each of these four approaches will speak to all the people in your congregation. By messaging your dream in various ways, you give others courage to dare to dream like Jesus with you. No matter which approach you take, let your faith in God, your passion for the dream, and your belief in your people show through. Those qualities will inspire every congregational culture.

Now that you have some ideas about how to message your dream most effectively for your people, let's look at another key piece of generating alignment in the next chapter. You'll need a rationale for your vision with compelling reasons to buy-in.

ALIGN Others to Your Dream

Identify Congregational Culture

Go to mydreamlikejesus.com. Download or continue completing the worksheets.

Alone or with a team, consider your congregation and identify the following aspects of your culture:

- **Get 'Er Done**
  What people or elements in your congregation fit this archetype?

- **Get 'Er Done With Fun**
  What people or elements in your congregation fit this archetype?

- **Get 'Er Done by Consensus**
  What people or elements in your congregation fit this archetype?

- **Get 'Er Done Right**
  What people or elements in your congregation fit this archetype?

Given the various archetypes present in your congregation which one or two shape the shape culture overall?

Identify Congregational Culture

- _____

- _____

- _____

- _____

- _____

CHAPTER EIGHT
Reasons and Rationale

The dictionary defines rationale as "a set of reasons or a logical basis for a course of action or a particular belief." Having a solid rationale is critical for the kind of clear communication that paves the way for people to get on board with the vision. At this point in the game, with congregational culture in mind, it's time for you to explain why and how they should. First, tell your people why this dream is important, game-changing, and in sync with Jesus' dream. Second, tell your people how it fits into the Kingdom and the call of your congregation. Third, tell your people why us and why now. Finally, tell them the stepping stones to accomplish it. Together, this line of reasoning forms your rationale.

In explaining your rationale, be intentional about the kind of reasons you give. For instance, be prepared to ground the vision in the message of the Bible. Did Jesus speak to the issues at hand? Did his life in some way demonstrate an appropriate response? What light does the Old Testament shed on this issue? For religious, spiritual, or faith-based leaders, this type of rationale is essential. When preparing your rationale, be sure to do your homework as various parts of the Bible can be used to justify almost anything.

Next, draw upon the needs of the world in making your case. What does the world hunger for that this vision provides? Likewise, what does your congregation hunger for that this vision answers? What resources does each provide? As theologian Karl Barth is quoted as saying, "Preach with the newspaper in one hand and the Bible in the other." [39]

Do feel free to include how the vision resonates with your inner knowing or intuitive understanding. This will certainly speak to some of your people. It's valid to include the spiritual promptings you receive. You are, after all, a spiritual leader. But don't stop there. Inner promptings in and of themselves won't be enough to cultivate the kind of buy-in you'll need to see this Jesus-like dream through to completion. Your rationale also has to make logical sense. No matter your personality or temperament, this is the time for facts, figures, and background information. Gather the hard data you'll need to make a compelling case for your vision.

A word to the wise: When it comes to talking about the how of your dream, you won't need every detail spelled out or every possible complication figured out. In fact, too much detail at this point can get in the way. Your listeners may lose the forest for the trees. Some folks will quarrel with your details instead of responding to the vision as a whole. On the other hand, you'll need to present some specifics or it will seem too big, too unfocused, or too undefined. Don't let either too many or too few details derail the process.

Let's look at an example. Let's say your Kingdom-inspired dream is "There's No Place Like Home." You envision that your congregation will partner with other faith communities as well as community agencies to provide safe haven for families displaced by natural disaster. As a result, you imagine your community will gain a heightened sense of gratitude for their own sense of place, even as they compassionately welcome in these new families. Because of the necessity of ongoing collaboration of the church folks with community agencies, you expect that new relationships will form, new friendships will be birthed, and a tighter-knit community will be the result. And of course, the new families that move

to your community will come to know it as their new home.
All of your lives will be the richer for it. Now, it's time to
build your rationale.

Why This? Let's say through your Bible reading and
study, you've discovered a persistent thread running through
both Old and New Testaments about showing kindness and
hospitality to aliens, strangers, widows, orphans, and the
poor. It seems to be a sign of God's Kingdom here on earth.
You're aware that right now many people are fleeing war,
violence, and natural disaster. They have no place to call
home. You've discovered that, according to the UN Council
on Refugees, for the first time since World War II the number
of refugees, asylum-seekers, and internally displaced people
worldwide has exceeded fifty million people. Many of them
are women and children. You know that Jesus himself was
a refugee at one point, fleeing the violence of Herod with his
mother and father. Likewise, the exodus from Egypt was a
story of people fleeing hardship for a better life. Through
Moses, God shepherded them through the desert to the
Promised Land. Thus, "There's No Place Like Home" is
biblical, topical, and highly practical.

Why Us? Let's say a very active refugee family in your
congregation comes from a country rocked by a devastating
earthquake. They speak the language fluently and have gladly
introduced their country's special foods into the life of the
church. The mother and her family have made you aware of
the plight of their people. You know that your church is particularly good at providing hospitality and caring for people who
are down and out. You also have property to house a family.
In the past, you have used it to successfully provide shelter for
homeless women. This may be the next logical step. Now, local
caring agencies are looking to partner with churches to help
settle displaced people. Besides, your prayer team has been
praying for God's dream to come to life through you. Since
your congregational culture is Get 'er Done with Consensus,
once they buy in, they won't let people fall through the cracks.

Why Now? You tell your people there is both a great need, and a great opportunity to put the faith of your forebears into practice. You can be part of a denominational campaign for compassion. Other churches around the country are stepping up to welcome people who suffered in this disaster. Your congregation and community can learn from their experiences and make a true difference for these uprooted families. It's a beautiful opportunity to shine the light of Christ into the world.

Stepping Stones to Realize the Dream

1. Establish a community-wide prayer team to undergird all your efforts.

2. Partner with the local ecumenical association, local caring agencies, and your denomination to identify a displaced family from this particular country.

3. Work together to apply to your respective denominations for grant monies which can support the family for up to six months.

4. Work with church trustees and community agencies to ready homes for the family or families.

5. Train congregants and community members to minister to displaced families new to your community and country.

6. Learn about their home country including holidays, culture, language, and history. Be prepared to draw upon their strengths.

7. Organize the congregation and community to cook meals, provide support, and offer friendship to the family when they arrive and for the next few months.

8. Be ready to learn from the family and be enriched by them, as well as to give to them.

9. Welcome the family in.

10. Partner with other churches and community organizations to plan a "There's No Place Like Home" festival

that celebrates your community and its strengths. Use this opportunity to introduce the integrate the family into the life of the community.

Your vision may be very different from this example. No matter the vision, preparing this kind of rationale will help you clearly communicate your big dream with others. It also readies you to create a well-organized message to present to your people.

Your message will need a logical beginning and end, and be laid out in such a way that the vision and the details all make sense. Include a visual and something people can take away with them. For instance, you may prepare a PowerPoint or shoot a video, and provide a handout or a flow chart to give people to follow along as you make your cake.

You may not be naturally built to present things in such a way. But if you are thinking, "This is hard work! I don't think like this or work like this," rest assured that putting the time and energy into this now will greatly help you later. You'll be able to communicate a clear, cohesive message that energizes and inspires people to get on board with you. Worried that you can't do this? Press on. "Culture-shifting" leaders not only build on their strengths, they also address their weaknesses. Many of the people we've mentored through *Creating a Culture of Renewal*® never imagined they could shepherd this sort of dream, yet to their great delight they found that they could. Remember that we've said a Jesus-like dream expands assumptions about what is possible. Getting this organized just may be the breakthrough for you!

Communicate, Communicate, Communicate

Now that you have your vision, understand how to message it for your people, and have organized a cohesive rationale, it's time to get the conversation started! These days the options are limitless. Consider the various ways churches communicate news worth sharing: worship services, letters, announcements (including printed, spoken, video, email, and social media posts), sermons, newsletter articles, devotions, Power Point presentations, banners, prayer, and presentations made to committees, teams, and community groups. Use each of these ways to get the message out, but don't stop there.

We know from the Gospels that not only did Jesus speak to others about his vision, but they spoke back. And how! Give people a chance to respond to your vision through panels, town hall meetings, small group sessions, and one-on-one conversations.

But remember, buy-in will take time. This isn't business as usual. You are undertaking a Kingdom-oriented shift with a visionary dream that expands assumptions about what is possible. Use every avenue you have to engage and re-engage people!

Let's take a look at how Jesus did it. Often, he rolled out his ideas over a meal (Luke 11:37-52, 14:1-24, 22:14-38). At other times, he spoke in front of large crowds (Luke 14:25-35). Frequently, he met his disciples in small group settings to engage in dialogue and answer their questions (Luke 11:1-13). In fact, it seems that Jesus cast his vision just about everywhere he went. Most notably, he composed a prayer that kept his dream in front of people every time they prayed it: "Thy Kingdom come, thy will be done, on earth as it is in heaven" (Matthew 6:10 NIV).

It's interesting that Jesus gained great alignment for his vision even though he often spoke in enigmatic parables and depended on people's innate spiritual ability to understand his message. I suspect people got on board with Jesus because of his remarkable actions – healings and miracles – even more than his words.

If you can pull it off at this point, healings and miracles will go a long way toward gaining alignment! If you're not there, try the old stand-by. Sit down with people and engage in presentations followed by genuine dialogue. Question and answer sessions, home gatherings, retreats, Bible studies, staff meetings, committee meetings, board or council meetings, men's and women's groups, youth group, annual meetings, panels, webinars, conference calls, and meals are especially appropriate settings for dialogue. And by all means, put it on your website, Facebook page, and in the bulletin. This list is by no means exhaustive. The point is to create a space where people feel comfortable talking openly. This varies by age, region of the country, congregational culture, ethnic culture, work schedule, and other expectations.

As you get ready for group discussions, keep two things in mind. First, be ready for the unexpected. Even though you have spent time preparing yourself, your people will raise issues you haven't thought of. They'll also offer praise and make connections you hadn't counted on.

Second, be receptive. The more receptive you are to comments, both positive and negative, the safer people will feel to engage in the process. In fact, staying open is especially important at this stage. The purpose of these conversations is to give people a chance to weigh in. This might mean they disagree with you, vehemently or subtly. Not always fun. But without the chance to weigh-in, people are much less likely to buy-in. Be ready to entertain their questions, and concerns, and even their challenges.

Please note that staying open doesn't mean you have to agree with others, like what they say, or take every suggestion. You don't. But you do have to listen closely to people's concerns. Take care not to interpret their comments as an assault on your person, your ministry, your calling, your relationship with God, your understanding of the future, your leadership qualities, or even your relationship with that person. Remember, you are stretching everyone here. Big dreams can ramp up anxiety. So, be patient. Be calm. Be confident. Be non-anxious. Be curious and playful. Above all, be prayed-up!

The key here is to communicate, communicate, communicate. Declare your dream until you know it by heart, until your kids can say it along with you, until you're sick of it. And most especially, say it until your people say it back to you. Or better yet, until they tell other people. That's when you'll know you're gaining their alignment.

Pastor David Madara's dream was to reduce the number of tragic deaths in his county. Part of his strategy was for all the churches to cooperate on a number of life-giving initiatives. A candidate for Sheriff was going door-to-door in the county to meet voters and share his platform. He knocked on the door of Marla, a member of David's congregation. "What are you doing to gather the churches together to reduce tragic deaths in our county?" she asked him. "My church is involved in doing a number of things," he responded. "No," she said, "churches," emphasizing the plural, "not just your church." Not only had Marla, a lay person, caught the vision, but she was busy sharing it with others. If David hadn't shared his vision widely, she couldn't either. The point is, don't skimp on this step of alignment.

Be sure to present the vision to the leadership board, the finance team, and the personnel committee. Don't forget worship, missions, the youth, young adult ministry, and the homebound. Do you have crafters, a preschool, or other groups that meet in your building? Share it with all of them and engage them in dialogue. You'll be surprised at the level of interest your Jesus-like dream garners.

There's one more thing to keep in mind. Not only do you need people's emotional buy-in, you'll also need the alignment of resources. Staff (whether volunteer or paid), monies, ministries, and time may need to be re-directed to accomplish the new life-giving dream you are inviting them into. This phase of alignment will take time, consideration, and prayer. Be patient, but don't give up. Build out your reasons and rationale with an eye to the resources that will be needed. Remember the power of prayer. Jesus encourages you to ask for whatever you need and then believe that you have received it. I encourage you to employ gutsy prayer as you continue to seek alignment.

Over the years I have presented many visions. At times, I have been surprised when someone I considered a friend openly questioned my premise or rationale. I have since learned it's not personal. After all, I am asking people to buy-in to something that will change the structure, expectations, and processes of "the way we do things." They have a right to speak up. In fact, I want them to voice their concerns. Chances are, they'll bring up something that will help us avoid unanticipated trouble or maximize outcomes. This shift in my reaction didn't happen overnight. It took some hard knocks. It also took maturing in faith, understanding, and emotional intelligence.

Chances are, you'll encounter pushback, too. I want you to be ready. In the next chapter, we'll take a closer look at how to mine it for unexpected blessings.

ALIGN Others to Your Dream

Create Your Rationale	
Go to mydreamlikejesus.com. Download or continue completing the worksheets. Alone or with a team, write out the following: ■ **Why This?** Why is this dream important to God? Your community? Your church? ■ **Why Us?** Why is this calling important for your congregation? ■ **Why Now?** What makes this dream important to undertake now? ■ **Stepping Stones** What big steps would be needed to realize the dream?	**Create Your Rationale** ■ _____ ■ _____ ■ _____ ■ _____ ■ _____

CHAPTER NINE

The Positive Power of Pushback

A few years back, I met with more than a dozen leaders, most of them pastors, in a beautiful wooded location when red and orange maple leaves lay nestled under a fresh dusting of snow. We were far from the crunch of day-to-day ministry. Our retreat location was safe and our conversations were relevant. We followed a process that had worked well in a variety of settings. Each of the fifteen leaders had personally signed up and paid their registration fee. By all accounts, they had bought in to the process and seemed to be personally committed to the work. This was "Congregational Intelligence," Track 1 of *Creating a Culture of Renewal*®. They were in it because they wanted to expand their thinking, to experience personal renewal, and to bring renewal to their congregations. We were off to a promising start. Or so I thought.

Then sessions grew strangely contentious. I said black, they said white. I said up, they countered down. I said possible, they shook their heads no: impossible. What was going on here? I worried that I was making leaps in logic that confused these leaders. I worried that the group facilitators were not seasoned enough. I worried that perhaps the group was too large. The truth is, I couldn't figure out what was going on; I was confounded.

I puzzled over this for the next six months as the group continued to meet and to contend. Over time, I realized the underlying problem. These leaders had already bought in more deeply to a different story. They worked in a system that promised change but didn't deliver, that promised spiritual care but focused on saving money, that declared visionary leadership but cultivated caution. They were embedded in the narrative of the system: We're in decline, not much can change; now it's just about managing risk. Why trust anything else? These faith-filled leaders had been deeply called by God but weren't ready for the leap of faith I coaxed them to.

One of the primary distinctions I bring to churches is the idea that like Jesus, you are not bound by circumstance. You are bigger than your circumstances. They continued to insist that they weren't. Circumstances were what they were. Their ministries were constrained by inflexible budgets, their congregations were small, and their populations were aging. What else could be done?

All of this conversation took place within a hidden context: their story that the system had failed them. Their context was no longer Jesus' calling on their life, but the lack of personal agency and professional support they experienced within the system.

While I expected excitement at the retreat, even cautious excitement, what I got was pushback. It showed up throughout the retreat in worry, anxiety, excessive questioning, and fault-finding. One of the participants was domineering, giving voice to what a few others felt but were afraid to say. But all of it was pushback against the idea that by shifting their perspectives the church itself could change. Lack of faith in the system eclipsed their faith in possibility. More than that, it eclipsed their belief in their own authority and agency.

They couldn't see it at the time, but their pushback against me and my ideas mirrored that of their congregations against them. It was just this sort of resistance that had worn down these very leaders. It was the reason they had come to the retreat in the first place. They were there to learn about renewal, yet they reflexively rehearsed their own resistance.

It's like that in the church. When you get resistance from the people you lead, it's easy to project that upon the people who supervise you. When you get resistance from above, you quench the flow of insight and bold action to the people you serve. When you get it from within, it constrains you from without. That's what happens when you let circumstances limit your faith and dictate your actions. It's what happens when you insist on seeing before believing.

I understand the worry. I know what it feels like to be up against a shrinking budget, declining worship attendance, and waning faith. I've experienced that in all three churches I pastored. But what's different about daring to dream like Jesus is that your currency is vision, not visible circumstances. Vision, by definition, assumes that both the issues and the solutions are bigger than you are, but neither is bigger than your creative partnership with God. As one sister visionary put it to me, "We have help from the fourth dimension to navigate the three-dimensional world."

Back to this group of spiritual leaders. We met again in the spring, some six months later, to complete Track 1 of *Creating a Culture of Renewal*®, and to celebrate how they had grown in their "Congregational Intelligence." Something was different this time. The air was clearer, the atmosphere lighter. While a few persisted in negative fault-finding, at least half of the group had made a significant shift. Actions that had seemed impossible six months earlier had proven possible. These leaders had caught the vision of renewal, embraced their own agency, and brought new perspectives back to their ministry settings. Wonderful new dynamics had emerged in their congregations. Adversarial relationships had softened. Harsh self-assessments had eased. Circular conversations about lack of money and scant involvement had branched off in new, fresh directions. One pastor had even called her bishop and aired long-suppressed fears and grievances. As a result, her health improved as remarkably as the quality of her ministry.

Fast forward five months. As the maple and oak leaves began to hint at a glorious fall, eight of the original fifteen re-convened for the next stage of learning: "Leadership Smarts", which is Track 2 of *Creating a Culture of Renewal®*. "We're sorry," Janet said, "about last year. We just didn't trust. It wasn't you. But we had no idea if this was really going to work or not. We've been disappointed before." Now I had their buy-in. Nine months later we met again to reflect, integrate, and celebrate. Their fears had transformed into faith. One by one, they shared remarkable results in their personal lives and their ministry settings. Stephan disclosed that while he had been pastoring for thirty years, this was the first time that he actually had acquired the skills to effectively lead. His lay leaders noticed and affirmed him. Miguel revealed that he had overcome the fear of people who were more direct and demanding than he. Instead of seeing them as bullies, he was now able to treat them as allies for a common purpose. For the first time in years, he was upping his game to engage them. Dahlia had completed an unfinished manuscript after twenty years of self-doubt. She even found a publisher. Ephedra had cut through confusion surrounding finances in her church, and in the process uncovered pressing health concerns among her leaders which had to be addressed, saving her congregation from two forms of potential chaos: financial and organizational.

Three months later, we met to begin the last segment of the *Creating a Culture of Renewal®* curriculum: "Culture Shift." All eight continued, working on their own visions inspired by what they already accomplished. Like doves released from cages, their visions began to take flight. Their congregations are taking wing too, inspired by their leaders' newfound skill and faith.

Here's the point of the story: even the best visions get pushback. Pushback doesn't mean you've got it wrong or you didn't sense the Spirit correctly. Nor does it mean they are wrong. In my case, it meant I was asking this group to play a bigger game than they were used to. It took time for them to test and try the process. Pushback can also be a sign there are dynamics at play that you're unaware of, or that you need a new way to present things, or finally that they have questions you don't yet have answers for.

Caught unaware, too many spiritual leaders get taken out at this stage of the game. Pushback feels like an attack, which undermines and sabotages everything you've already done. My colleague Michael is getting a ton of pushback on something that isn't even happening yet. He is walking a tight rope between, "I must be wrong since they are pushing hard against me," and "But I know God is leading this way."

It is imperative for you to expect pushback and be able to confidently say, "Pushback does not necessarily mean I'm wrong." It's also good for you to remember that it isn't YOU personally that they are pushing against. Your people would push regardless of who brings the idea. Even necessary change is uncomfortable.

A few years back, I mentored a Lay Leader, let's call him Chance, who worked closely with the Mission Team. Guided by the Holy Spirit, in consultation with trusted leaders, he crafted a bold, inspiring, Kingdom-oriented vision. He prayed and received confirmation. He'd done his homework, which made him all the more defensive when the objections started. It got to the point where every time someone raised an objection, his critique-o-meter spiked. He experienced their questions as a personal attack. The more attacked he felt, the more he closed himself off and hunkered down. The more he hunkered down, the more shut out and shut down they felt. It was quickly turning into a no-win situation. Finally, he realized that their questions weren't personal attacks. Once he started to calm down, he became more receptive to their questions and concerns. As he worked through the process, he discovered what I call pushback paradoxes.

Pushback Paradox #1: Pushback is a sign of deep interest, not lack of interest. Because your big dream will introduce new dynamics and change the way you do things, people want to have their ideas, concerns, or refinements included in it. Take their objections as a sign of interest. This shift in your perspective will set the stage for a more productive process.

Pushback Paradox #2: Pushback is a sign of lack of understanding, not of rejection. At this point in the game, people will need details. Don't shoot from the hip; rather, take time to organize your thoughts. Help them understand how it will all come together. Be patient with people, and communicate, communicate, communicate.

Pushback Paradox #3: Pushback is a sign of wanting greater involvement, not less. Many people will want to have their fingerprints on a major change in the church. Suggestions and objections actually help them buy in to your vision.

People enjoy change as long as it's the kind of change they like, at the time they desire it, and if things turn out the way they want them to. Your vision, by necessity, implies change is on its way. While it's likely to be good change, no one is thrilled about change that is beyond their control.

One judicatory I worked with rolled out their new vision after a period institutional preparation. It was inspiring, comprehensive, and promised a new, refreshed state of affairs. But as they aligned monies to the new vision, they had to say no to projects they had previously funded. While it was a positive change overall, it didn't feel so positive for the people whose budgets were cut or whose committees were reconfigured. Yet, the judicatory absolutely needed to make this change. To their great credit, they even found a way to deal with the unhappy people and the organizational upset that change would bring. Listening was the key. "We know you've listened to us," the disaffected and un-funded committee members said, "and that's making this transition that much easier." When you contemplate making a big change, do likewise. Hear people's concerns, worries, fears, grief, as well as their excitement. If people get to weigh in, they are much more likely to buy in. The truth is, people are less afraid of change than they are of being disenfranchised. Hearing them out will go a long way towards building trust in the midst of change.

Check to see if you are criticizing or challenging every new idea or tweak suggested. If you are, take a deep breath, close your mouth, open your ears, and listen to what they have to say. Really listen. Don't just wait to slip in your rebuttals. Even if you don't ultimately incorporate other ideas, being heard has a calming effect. It reduces anxiety, buoys morale, and lets people know they matter. If you listen closely enough, your people will tell you what's missing to make the vision a new and shining reality.

The truth is, pushback is necessary for buy-in. Without pushback, you can't be sure that people have had a chance to fully consider and think through the new direction God is calling you to. Better to have it surface now than simmer just below the surface. Pushback is much easier to address head on than when it slides into an undercurrent of murmuring resistance.

You've heard it said, "Where there is no vision, the people will perish" (Proverbs 29:18). Now consider this. Without push-back and the buy-in that comes from it, the leader will perish, because they'll be in it all by themselves. Your dream is worth persevering through pushback.

As beautiful as the Kingdom dream was, even Jesus got

push back, and lots of it. Not everyone liked his ideas. Rome was threatened by his talk of kingship and Jewish leaders were afraid his outsize influence would initiate a Roman crackdown. Some wanted to silence him, others wanted to jail him, still others wanted to kill him. But at the same time that Jesus' detractors grew in number, so did his followers.

Jesus took time away on the lake and in the wilderness to be with God to get re-centered. When you get pushback, you may need a break from folks, too. But just like the crowds wouldn't let Jesus alone, don't you stay away. Your people need you: your leadership, your vision, your tenacity, your faith. Above all, they need your presence.

You may wonder how it'll all turn out. At times, Jesus wondered the same as he prayed in the garden, "Let this cup pass from me." It was easy to sense his resignation, or perhaps his surrender, as he continued on in prayer, "Not my will but yours" (Matthew 26:39). As godforsaken as he felt in the moment, and as horrific as the cross was, I'm so glad he persevered. If he hadn't, there would be no resurrection, no story of new life. I encourage you to stay with it, too. Your people are counting on you to be with them as the old is passing away, so that something new can be birthed.

Finally, I want to leave you with these thoughts as you engage the pushback and navigate change. Pray for each other. Ask God what you can do to ease the grief of change as you forward your Jesus-like dream. Ask how you can be kind toward those who misunderstand you and do good to those whom you fear may hate you. Ask to see things from another's perspective. In situations like these, I pray: God prepare our hearts and minds for each other.

It's also important to ask *how* questions, not *why* questions. Why questions put people on the defensive. How questions encourage people to think creatively. For instance: How does this change impact you? Not: Why won't you go along with this?

Assume the best about others, not the worst. If you catch yourself thinking that yours is the only right way, this principle will be hard to adopt.

Now that you have learned how to align others to your dream, it's time for the next step--how to bring the dream to life!

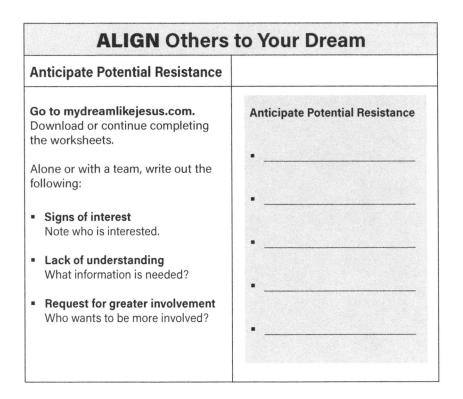

ALIGN Others to Your Dream

Anticipate Potential Resistance

Go to mydreamlikejesus.com. Download or continue completing the worksheets.

Alone or with a team, write out the following:

- **Signs of interest**
  Note who is interested.

- **Lack of understanding**
  What information is needed?

- **Request for greater involvement**
  Who wants to be more involved?

Anticipate Potential Resistance

- _____

- _____

- _____

- _____

- _____

PART 4
Realize the Dream

*In the third step of the DARE model, **R** is for Realize the dream. First, learn how to make the dream a reality. Second, operate in Jesus' name. And third, acknowledge and celebrate how far the dream has brought you.*

CHAPTER TEN
Make the Dream Reality

Once you begin to dream like Jesus, and dare to speak your dream out loud, you've already begun to usher the seemingly impossible into the realm of the possible. It's amazing what simply articulating a vision can do to bring it into fruition. While speaking it out loud in itself takes courage, you've gone beyond that. You've dialogued about it with your people, gotten their feedback, addressed their pushback, and begun to gain their alignment.

Now, you're ready for the third step in the DARE process: to realize the dream. This is where the future becomes reality. It's time to gear up to implement the vision. In order to fully bring the dream to reality in such a way that you're not doing all the work yourself, you'll need a strategy for the impossible to become possible. Creating a strategy that has broad buy-in means the difference between, "We already tried that and it didn't work," and "We didn't think we could do it, but we did!"

Jesus had a definite strategy to realize his dream. He delegated his authority to his friends and followers. In fact, it's not even Jesus who actually fulfilled his dream. It was his people.

> *⁵These twelve Jesus sent out with the following instructions: "Go nowhere among the Gentiles, and enter no town of the Samaritans, ⁶ but go rather to the lost sheep of the house of Israel· ⁷ As you go, proclaim the good news, 'The Kingdom of heaven has come near.' ⁸ Cure the sick, raise the dead, cleanse the lepers, cast out demons.*
>
> **Matthew 10:5-8a (NRSV)**

Do you see it? Jesus empowered, authorized, and dispatched twelve others to enact his dream. They announced the Kingdom and manifested it through miracles. That they collaborated with him indicates their buy-in. It means Jesus had successfully cast the vision and communicated it to them, and given them an engaging way to participate.

> *You received without payment; give without payment. ⁹ Take no gold, or silver, or copper in your belts, ¹⁰ no bag for your journey, or two tunics, or sandals, or a staff; for laborers deserve their food.*
>
> **Matthew 10:8b-10 (NRSV)**

As specific as he was, though, Jesus did not fall into micro-managing. He demonstrated trust in their ability to discern the nature of the people they would encounter and to handle themselves well.

¹¹ Whatever town or village you enter, find out who in it is worthy, and stay there until you leave. ¹² As you enter the house, greet it. ¹³ If the house is worthy, let your peace come upon it; but if it is not worthy, let your peace return to you. ¹⁴ If anyone will not welcome you or listen to your words, shake off the dust from your feet as you leave that house or town.

Matthew 10:11-14 (NRSV)

Long before Jesus – the master, healer, and teacher – even made the rounds, his dream was being realized. This is key. Jesus skillfully brought his dream to life through his people: the hallmark of apostolic leadership. Effective leadership taps into the hopes, dreams, and agency of others. The Twelve had now moved from discipleship into apostleship. No longer were they just followers, they became active agents of his dream. In fact, it had become their dream.

But bringing new dreams to life is not a linear process. It's a spiral that redoubles and comes around again. Watch how Jesus demonstrated this principle.

Now when Jesus had finished instructing his twelve disciples, he went on from there to teach and proclaim his message in their cities.

Matthew 11:1 (NRSV)

Did you catch that? Jesus had just sent off his twelve closest followers – fully empowered and authorized – to enact his dream, and then he was off to share his dream, build alignment for it and bring it to reality among brand new people! Powerful dreams are like that. They compel you, energize you, and pull you forward. This was not drudgery for Jesus. It was his passion and purpose in life (Matthew 4:23-25, Mark 1:35-39, Luke 4:42-44). It was the reason he got out of bed in the morning. His dream made him unstoppable!

After Jesus sent out The Twelve to go into the towns around them, he was ready to ramp things up. He then sent out seventy-two people who have already caught his vision (the number is seventy in some versions). Then watch what Jesus did in Luke 10:1:

After this the Lord appointed seventy others and sent them on ahead of him in pairs to every town and place where he himself intended to go.

He started by giving them his rationale, found in Matthew 10:2-3:

[2] The harvest is plentiful, but the laborers are few; therefore ask the Lord of the harvest to send out laborers into his harvest. [3] Go on your way. See, I am sending you out like lambs into the midst of wolves.

Then, he assigned them specific action items along with some instructions in Matthew 10:4-9:

[4]Carry no purse, no bag, no sandals; and greet no one on the road. [5]Whatever house you enter, first say, 'Peace to this house!' [6]And if anyone is there who shares in peace, your peace will rest on that person; but if not, it will return to you. [7]Remain in the same house, eating and drinking whatever they provide, for the laborer deserves to be paid. Do not move about from house to house. [8]Whenever you enter a town and its people welcome you, eat what is set before you; [9]cure the sick who are there, and say to them, 'The Kingdom of God has come near to you.'

Interestingly, even those townspeople who didn't buy in to Jesus' vision would still be made aware of it.

[10]But whenever you enter a town and they do not welcome you, go out into its streets and say,

110

[11]"Even the dust of your town that clings to our feet, we wipe off in protest against you. Yet know this: the Kingdom of God has come near.'

Luke 10: 10-11 (NSRV)

He had some choice words for those who don't buy in.

[21]"Woe to you, Chorazin! Woe to you, Bethsaida! For if the deeds of power done in you had been done in Tyre and Sidon, they would have repented long ago, sitting in sackcloth and ashes. [22]But at the judgment it will be more tolerable for Tyre and Sidon than for you. [23]And you, Capernaum, will you be exalted to heaven? No, you will be brought down to Hades."

Matthew 11:21-23 (NSRV)

Jesus made it clear that these seventy-two people would enact the Kingdom. In other words, realization of the dream of the Kingdom had begun.

"Whoever listens to you listens to me; whoever rejects you rejects me; but whoever rejects me rejects him who sent me."

Luke 10:16 (NSRV)

Just as clear is that these seventy-two people bought in to the vision of the Kingdom—spiritually and emotionally, which empowered them to heal the sick, announce the Kingdom and cast out demons—the action items Jesus delegated to them. Their sense of accomplishment was palpable here.

The seventy-two returned with joy and said, "Lord, even the demons submit to us in your name"

Luke 10:17 (NSRV)

You want your people to come home rejoicing, too. That means you need a strategy, and a team to carry it out. Here's how Rev. Steve Trout built a team. Remember his vision, "A Hunger to End Hunger?" Steve did three main things to unify people around an inspiring vision. First, he preached on this effort throughout the fall to his congregation, getting their buy-in to the vision. Second, he held Bible studies throughout Lent to educate his congregation on Biblical sources for engaging with people who had less resources. Third, he gathered a cadre of now-interested congregants who stepped forward to help him reach out. They reached out to other like-minded folks from outreach agencies in the spring and summer. This strategy worked well.

Okay, tell the truth here. Are you used to doing things by yourself? Do you prefer it? Do you have a hard time including others in the process? Let me remind you that flying solo won't work well with a Jesus-like dream. Just like Jesus had people, you need people, too. If a Jesus-like dream is bigger than you are, then it simply can't be accomplished by one person or even a few people. You're going to need help to realize this dream.

How are you with team building? All too often, leaders have unconscious self-limiting beliefs such as the buried belief that you don't deserve to ask for help, or that no one is interested or available to help you. As novelist Scott Turow famously observed, "Who are we but the stories we tell ourselves, about ourselves, and believe?"[40] What stories do you tell yourself? If you believe you have to do it all yourself, this belief not only limits you, it limits the faith and involvement of the people around you. When you don't give others a way to participate, they are unable to exercise their gifts or contribute to something larger than themselves. "You have not because you ask not," Jesus reminded us in James 4:3.

On the other hand, you may be quite intentional about not asking for help. If you don't want to risk others doing it "wrong" please consider whether control may be your issue.

The desire for perfection is admirable, however, perfection-ism limits the exercise of gifts and faith of your people. If perfection is the goal, Jesus would have every reason to do it all himself: every miracle, every healing, every proclamation. But if he could risk help from the twelve, the seventy-two, and so forth, so can you.

As I said before, if Jesus tried to do it all himself the vision would have died with him. Then where would we be? Doing everything isn't leading. It's simply doing everything. Jesus delegated; so can you.

Surprisingly, Jesus has said that you would do even greater things than he did. How on earth could that be true? I'll tell you this, it can't happen if you don't share the risks and rewards of this work with others. If Jesus could risk others doing miracles in his name, you can risk it, too! Trust your vision. Trust your co-workers in the Lord. Trust the process. True, it may not come out as planned. In fact, it may come out even better.

Next, let's look at strategy. Strategy is what moves your impossible dream into the realm of the possible. Whether creating a strategy is easy for you or hard, it's got to be done in order to realize your Jesus-like dream. The key component of a workable strategy to realize your dream is a set of goals. Step by step goals help everyone stay on track and ensure that you are working toward a common vision. If you created a stepping stones portion for your rationale, build on that by filling in the blanks between each step. With your team, add in who will do what. Don't forget to add in dates for accom-plishing the various goals.

Some of you may be thinking, "I fly by the seat of my pants. I don't do step by step." Okay, that may be true for you. But chances are, your people do. If you're going to actually bring this bold and beautiful vision of yours to life, and to manifest the Kingdom in your corner of the world, you need those people. And they need goals with a step by step plan to accomplish them. Mapping out the goals may feel energizing or ponderous, but either way this process needn't drag things out.

Being a Champion

Now that you've put together a strategy to realize your dream, it's time to advocate for its implementation. You'll need to create the right environment for the strategies to be carried out and for your team to succeed. That's where you being a champion comes in. In the book, *The Work of Leaders: How Vision, Alignment and Execution Will Change the Way You Lead,* authors Julie Straw, Barry Davis, Mark Scullard, and Susie Kukkonen describe what it means to be a champion.

"A champion is:

- A defender of the time a team needs to work through solutions
- A proponent of a better structure or plan to help people achieve
- An advocate for the work and workers, praising and offering feedback
- A lobbyist for adequate resources and ongoing support
- A booster who provides the necessary momentum, drive, or resources."

Championing the vision is the difference between seeing your dream come to life and seeing it recede into the past, unfulfilled. I can't overstate its importance to realizing the vision. I know because when I look in the rearview on my years of local church ministry, I can see the difference between visions I actively championed, and those I neglected. In particular, I remember one beautification project gone wrong.

I had a vision to plant trees and beautify the barren

property on which this little Wyoming church stood. Enthusiastically, people gathered around the idea. I knew I had buy-in because trees and fencing were donated. An early spring Saturday was set for planting the trees. Folks were excited! But we lacked a real plan for what would happen next, like watering and follow up care. Lots of trees got planted, but almost none of them survived. Over the next several years, their brown boughs served as a living, or rather dead, reminder of championing the cause. In fact, the property looked less beautiful with the dead trees dotting it than it had before.

It wasn't until years later when I learned about championing a vision that I realized how I could have handled the project differently. Yes, I cast the vision. Yes, I got buy-in. But I failed as a leader because I wasn't there to bring the dream into reality. I figured the details would take care of themselves. Had I been more attentive, I would have been aware of the holes in the plan, such as no provision being made for watering the trees. Instead, I was off to the next idea. That lack of championing the tree planting made the difference between a sustainable landscape and one that looked more barren than before. It wasn't enough to talk the idea into existence and to align people to the dream. Those trees and the people needed a defender, a proponent, an advocate, a lobbyist, and a booster. In the same way, your dream, your people, and your strategy need you to see them through.

Now that you have seen the importance of strategy, it's time to take courageous action to bring the dream to life!

REALIZE the Dream	
Map Your Strategy	
Go to mydreamlikejesus.com. Download or continue completing the worksheets. Alone or with a team, write out the following: • **Who?** Who needs to be involved? • **What?** What actions will they take? • **How?** How will they accomplish them? • **When?** When will each action be accomplished?	**Map Your Strategy** • _____ • _____ • _____ • _____ • _____

CHAPTER ELEVEN
In Jesus' Name

As disciples and apostles of Jesus Christ, you are given the powerful words, "In Jesus' name." You pray in his name, act in his name, minister in his name, dream, get buy-in, and champion dreams into reality in his name. That's what the church is all about, isn't it?

Jesus made things happen. Count up the number of miracle stories in the Gospels and beyond. He was on a roll! In fact, he was known to heal one person while on the way to heal another. He never missed an opportunity to play full out, engage a crowd, teach a lesson, or encourage his friends and followers. Jesus was always on the move, a rolling stone which gathered no moss.

Jesus' pace made sense. After all, he only had three years to gather students, instill his message in them, gain their buy-in, and bring his Kingdom message into reality! That's not a lot of time when you're out to change the world. He had work to do.

Sometimes you pretend that you have all the time in the world to get things done. You space out meetings a month at a time, reluctant to "bother" people with the work of the church. You don't go out of our way to let people know you have noticed and missed their presence, or even that you love them. But life changes in an instant. Today is the day you have to advance the dream. There is no other day.

This is important to remember when it comes to bringing your Jesus-like dream to life. Rev. Deborah was just getting started on some really great outreach ministry in her church when the Bishop called and said, "I'd like for you to serve in a larger capacity." Whoosh. Just like that, her opportunity to make a difference in that particular church was coming to a close.

Joe, a committed lay person, was rolling along beautifully, doing incredible work in his church. He was studying to take on an advanced leadership role when all of a sudden, his son was in a terrible accident and required long term care. He and his partner packed up and moved to take care of the young man. The point is we don't know how long we have. We plan. Yet, life continues to swirl around us.

This is it, folks. This is the time to get going, not to kick back and rest on your laurels. In fact, this is the time to drive it up a notch. Nothing matters more than bringing your Jesus-like dream to life. The self-defeating refrain, "We tried that and it didn't work," is born or dies precisely at this critical juncture. It all depends on how vigorously you champion the dream. Operating with a sense of urgency is a key dynamic here. Urgency emphasizes the value of your vision and the positive impact it will have on the people and world around you. It also prevents people from falling by the wayside, and important details from falling through the cracks.

Think about it. Your people have risked their hope, their creativity, their time, their money, and their imagination with you. Don't disappoint them or waste social capital by not continuing to call them to their greatness. Involving them in bringing the dream to reality is much more than recruiting volunteers or getting someone to do stuff you don't want to do. It's inviting them to see their greatness as a gift from God to empower others and call others to their greatness. This, dear leader, is discipling. Keep the Jesus-like dream before them and keep things moving so that this vision comes to fruition.

Trenda was big on big ideas. One of them was integrating autistic youth and young adults more fully into the life of the community. She gathered church and community stakeholders and wowed them with her vision. They bought in. Fully aligned, they worked together to create a beautiful strategy that they were eager to implement. Trenda was thrilled.

> **"Today is the day you have to advance the dream."**

One of the first steps in their strategy was to begin a worship service especially designed to gracefully and sensitively integrate people along the autism spectrum into the flow of worship. First, they tried beta versions. Autistic participants and advocates gave them helpful feedback. They worked through the issues that needed to be addressed and prepared for the next service, adjustments in place. It was all very exciting. Trenda still championed her "dream team," as she called them, and the worship service, but at the same time was being pulled into some new directions.

When the time came for the big launch, several members of the team weren't available. Work and family commitments had taken precedence. Even with the assurance of key stakeholders, the rest of the team resisted moving forward. They wanted to wait for the whole team to be together to begin. Meanwhile, Trenda herself was already on to the next big idea. Without her leadership, the team had no one to keep them together and provide momentum. The launch service was canceled. The rest of the strategy lay dormant until the team could come back together. But no one else with Trenda's passion or influence emerged to reconstitute the team so they could push forward to realize their dream. As you can imagine, the team scattered, and their plans were abandoned.

When word got around to the key stakeholders and supporters, they were disappointed. Disappointment hardened into resentment which finally morphed into resignation. Like a dark cloud, it settled in and obscured the community's previous hopefulness. Last I heard, that dark cloud was still there, some seven years after the fact.

What actually happened here? While Trenda had great ideas, the ability to build alignment, gather a dream team, and empower them to strategize a plan, she bailed at the last minute. And so did her team. Bottom line: Trenda lacked follow through. Just when her team needed her to pick up the pace, she was gone. Her dream was never realized.

Pastor Dan was laid back. A different kind of leader than Trenda, he was afraid to offend or push people too hard lest they burn out. It wasn't in his nature to risk everything. He felt he'd already risked quite a lot in terms of the visioning process by pushing for the idea of a city-wide interfaith prayer initiative. Yes, people had gotten on board, but it had been quite a haul. There had been some discontent and push back. While he came to understand that pushback was a natural part of gaining buy-in, frankly Dan was a bit scared. He worried that if he kept pushing them there would be a revolt. So, he maintained a low profile, stopped talking about the vision, and took a long breather before getting ready to talk about implementing the goals that would accomplish the vision. In the meantime, people started falling away. Dan was hurt and shocked when even some of his main supporters dropped out. He took it as a vote of no confidence in him and in the vision. He assumed he had rocked the boat too much and had pushed his people too hard. Given that, he made plans to leave.

After his departure, the personnel committee met with their regional superintendent to talk about what they were looking for in their next pastor. It was then that several of Dan's former supporters commented on how disappointed they were the vision never came to pass. Their disappointment was not that Dan had pushed them. They found that invigorating. They felt like they were finally doing something. They were disappointed that he seemed to lose interest in his own vision. After that, all the steam that had been building dissipated. What none of them could see was that Dan's lack of drive caused the dream of the prayer initiative to collapse around him. They weren't the ones who stopped caring. Nor did he, for that matter. But now the pastor is stuck with a story that people don't want to change, that he can't cast a vision, and that he had pushed too hard. They, on the other hand, are stuck with a story of how they tried to do something new but it didn't work, and that nothing could ever change in their church.

Can you relate to either of these stories? Are you like Trenda or Dan? If so, decide now to transform the way you normally do things. Lean into your weaknesses, until they become reliable strengths. Don't ask your people to transform the way they do things and take risks for the sake of the Kingdom if you won't. Lead by example. Operate in Jesus' name.

Then, take advantage of the buy-in you have gained and don't let up until the dream is fully implemented. Nothing will please your people more than seeing the vision come to fruition, the dream realized. This experience will deepen their trust in God, expand their self-confidence, heighten their appreciation of each other, and re-invigorate their commitment to the church. Bottom line: it will cause them to see how faith really does move mountains.

Jesus moved purposefully and intentionally through dream to alignment to realizing the Kingdom over the course of his three-year ministry. As I write this, it's Holy Week. I'm thinking about Jesus setting his face toward Jerusalem. As difficult as that was for him, I imagine he had great peace, too. For as he moved toward the cross, his Kingdom vision had already begun to be implemented. Think about it. He had already sent out the twelve, already sent out the seventy-two, already moved on and spoken of his dream in new areas and gathered new people. Those crowds who gathered to meet him on Palm Sunday were not passive supporters. They were active proponents of his vision. Jesus had a lot of folks who bought into the dream of the Kingdom. While some of them may have gotten scared and betrayed him, there is no hard evidence, by the way, that the same people who extolled him later cried for his crucifixion. That's a matter of homiletical flair and rhetorical interpretation. The point is, by the time Jesus' end came, he had already done his work to ensure that the dream would live on after him.

When Jesus charged his supporters with the Great Commission (Matthew 28:19-20) – to share his vision far and wide – they knew exactly what he was talking about. They were ready to go out and make disciples, to baptize, and to teach. They had been schooled in it for three years. And they already had a hand in implementing it. There was nothing left to chance at the end. How will it be for you?

Trenda bailed out just when things were getting good, and her team fell apart. Pastor Dan listened to his insecurities and they led him astray. Don't bail out. Don't listen to your insecurities. Instead, reclaim your authority and move into your agency. Pray for Holy Spirit guidance, steady your eye on the dream, work your strategy, and keep going.

Regular meetings help. Don't space them far apart because you will lose momentum. In fact, the more often you meet, the shorter and more focused each meeting can be. At the same time, give yourselves enough time to make a good plan and to think through what needs to be done next.

Together, anticipate cause and effect, plan for contingencies, think through what could go wrong, and eliminate risk. Also think about what could go well and right. What new opportunities could arise from this dream coming to life? Include plans to jump on those opportunities so you can keep the momentum going.

While you want your plans be vigorous and focused, don't

get stuck in the planning-to-do-something stage. Resist analysis paralysis. Let me repeat: resist analysis paralysis! Forgo the myth of perfection and move things forward. You can't know everything before you finally say, "Go." But your plans will help you deal with what you encounter along the way precisely because you will have thought through what could go right and what could go wrong. Seek help so as not to get mired in minutiae and to sidestep quicksand.

Once you have a plan, remember to stay in communication! Consistent and timely communication keeps planning on track and allows for real-time analysis. Regular communication also helps people feel like they are a part of things.

When you are in the phase of realizing the dream, it's easy to get overwhelmed with the number of things to do, the number of people you could put your attention on, and the number of ways each day could go. For me, the best days are those with a plan. Sometimes it's as simple as a monthly plan and a daily checklist. You may have a seasonal plan which not only relates to worship and ministries of the church but keeps the larger dream in mind at all times. Where are you headed? What one or two things will absolutely advance the goal, the vision, the ministry, the Kingdom? Prioritize those. What's not necessary or simply a time waster? You may have people like that. Or projects. Or worries. Reduce the amount of time you spend on each one of them.

The more focus you put on bringing your Jesus-like dream to life, the more you'll be setting the stage for a life-giving culture shift!

Jesus spent a great deal of time sharing his dream, educating his disciples about it, empowering them to carry it out, and then leading them through the paces of bringing it to life. That doesn't mean everything went smoothly and without a hitch. In fact, some of the most memorable stories about Jesus include his course corrections.

Course Corrections

Jesus addressed problems of ego. When an argument arose among his followers about which among them was the greatest disciple, Jesus used the littlest one around him to make a point. Putting a small child next to him, Jesus pointed out,

> *"Whoever welcomes this child in my name welcomes me, and whoever welcomes me welcomes the one who sent me; for the least among all of you is the greatest."*
>
> **Luke 9:48 (NSRV)**

Jesus was equally creative in addressing the problem of small-minded faith, and the recurring fear it brought up. Once out on the Sea of Galilee, a storm came up quickly while Jesus slept in the boat. The disciples, fearing for their lives, woke him up. It's a matter of faith, he said, as he calmed the stormy waters with his voice. The men around him were amazed,

> *"What sort of man is this, that even the winds and the sea obey him?"*
>
> **Matthew 8:27 (NSRV)**

He addressed problems of priorities as when the sisters Mary and Martha welcomed Jesus and his entourage of disciples into their home. Martha, mindful of being hospitable, got busy preparing for all her guests. Meanwhile her sister, Mary, was content to sit and listen to Jesus. When Martha scolded Mary through Jesus, Jesus returned the gentle scolding by letting Martha know that her worries were unnecessary; that it was okay to simply sit and be with Jesus (Luke 10:38-42).

You can see that Jesus didn't shy away from addressing problems. Nor did he neglect noticing what went well. He told the "sinful woman," who anoints his feet with oil, "Your sins are forgiven; your faith has save you; go in peace" (Luke 7:50).

Granted, it wasn't gushing praise, but he did acknowledge her positive behaviors.

He blessed Simon Peter after he responded appropriately to this question, "Who do you say that I am?" Simon Peter responded,

> *16 "You are the Messiah, the Son of the living God." 17 And Jesus answered him, "Blessed are you, Simon son of Jonah! For flesh and blood has not revealed this to you, but my Father in heaven. 18 And I tell you, you are Peter, and on this rock I will build my church, and the gates of Hades will not prevail against it."*

Matthew 16:16-18 (NSRV)

Again, not a lot of warm fuzzies. But the point is, Jesus did tell people when they got things wrong and when they got things right. He was willing to speak up to give feedback. In the same way, you'll have to speak up, too. If you won't insist on things going well, or addressing problems when they don't, then who will? As the authors of *The Work of Leaders* note, appropriate feedback keeps people engaged, motivated, and on track. Not giving feedback leaves people feeling direction-less, uninspired, and disengaged.

Before Peter, Andrew, James, and the rest of the men and women who met Jesus, got on board with his vision, they didn't have a full sense of their own capacities. It wasn't until Jesus dared them with his dream, and challenged them to fulfill it, did they fully live into their greatness. Because Jesus and his dream dared them to be their very best, they grew into his vision of them.

Bringing a dream to life takes courage. Operating in Jesus' name includes taking action now and offering course corrections. Even in the face of fear. Especially in the face of fear. When you take courageous action, you set the stage for one of the most overlooked steps to realizing the dream—celebration! Read on to see what's next.

REALIZE the Dream

Take Courageous Action	
Go to mydreamlikejesus.com. Download or continue completing the worksheets. Alone or with a team, write out the courageous actions you need to take: ▪ **Action 1** ▪ **Action 2** ▪ **Action 3** ▪ **Action 4** ▪ **Action 5**	**Take Courageous Action** ▪ _____ ▪ _____ ▪ _____ ▪ _____ ▪ _____

CHAPTER TWELVE
Celebrate the Dream

"We're always on to the next thing," one lay leader confided to me. "At least that's how the lay people in church see it. We're ever on to the latest, greatest solution for church growth."

"Do you ever pause and celebrate what you have already accomplished?" I asked.

"No."

His answer got me thinking. I thought back to the congregation I worked with that transformed its entire ministry from carbon heavy to carbon zero. Their light and heating bills went down. Their carbon footprint went down. They were living their dream. Or so I thought. "How are people responding?" I asked the leader who spearheaded the effort. "I'll bet they're excited!" "The people?" he said, sounding confused. "I don't think we've really told the people." What a missed opportunity! Don't make the same mistake.

At this point in your work, it's time to celebrate the dream. You have come so far. You have been sharing the vision, aligning others to it, and bringing it into reality. You may know all this. But if your people don't, then something is missing. It's time to celebrate!

Repeatedly, Jesus told stories of celebration. The woman

who lost the coin and found it, the shepherd who found the one lost sheep, the father who celebrated the return of his son. Now that you've joined the circle of visionaries and found the hope that was once lost, it's time for you to kill the fatted calf and throw a party for you and your friends.

"But we're not done yet," you cry. No matter. Even though your initiatives aren't complete, even though there is more work to be done, please don't skip this all-important step. It will give your people a necessary opportunity to reflect and rejoice. After all, they have been engaged in hard work. It's not easy to expand your assumptions about what is possible, buy in to a vision that isn't assured of working, and overcome inertia to implement a Kingdom-oriented dream. Especially if your congregation is comprised of the Get 'er Done by Consensus and Get 'er Done Right archetypes. You've asked them to come way out of their comfort zone. To the extent that they have, deserves celebration.

I have often wondered if people would respond more favorably to the risky work of dreaming like Jesus if they were aware of how much they are actually accomplishing. You have pushed people. Now let them rejoice.

There's nothing inherently wrong or anti-Christian with savoring our successes. Paul says we are to rejoice in all things. Usually, we think about rejoicing even when things are tough. I am suggesting that you rejoice when your hearts are in the right place, when your courage has been awakened, and when you are trying things you have never done before.

Living the Dream

One church that was celebrating its successes instituted a "Living the Dream" campaign. Each Sunday in worship, they took three to five minutes to celebrate how the dream was being realized around them. One week, they might show a video interview with someone from the community. Another week, it might be a live testimony from a church member involved in the dream. And yet another week, it might be a list of specific thanksgivings lifted up in prayer and praise, or a PowerPoint set to music with images of their dream in action.

Interestingly enough, this church never seemed to run out of things to say. Because each week that they shared good news with the congregation, their campaign strengthened the vision, deepened alignment, and revealed one more way they could further realize the dream.

Would you like to launch a Living the Dream celebration campaign in your congregation? Start by counting the tangible things that are coming to pass. For instance, how many new ministries have you launched since you started to dream like Jesus? How many new lives have you touched? How many prayers have been prayed? How many new relationships have been started? It's important to count and celebrate tangible wins, however small.

Harder to measure but equally important are the intangible wins. For instance, how many members and volunteers have been re-energized? How many callings to the ministry have been reclaimed? How many people have grown in their faith? How much despair has been averted? The truth is, you can't know these things unless you make space for collecting and telling these stories.

As the semi-frenetic pastor of an active congregation, I had habitually pushed on to the next thing. And the next. And the next. Driven by both the joy of accomplishment and the fear of boredom, I pushed my people, too. "Rev. Rebekah," my active lay leader sheepishly confessed to me one day, "we're tired. We need a rest. Can't we just stop for a bit and see how far we have actually come?"

When Jesus went into the wilderness to pray, we have no idea what he prayed. But we do know one thing. He paused. Surely something good and life-giving happened during that time.

Look around at all that has happened since you began to dream like Jesus. What could you celebrate in your congregation or ministry setting? Look for what you are doing well, and then emphasize it. Perspectives shift when we focus on what is going well.

I remember several years ago listening to a panel of General Conference delegates report on what had happened at the gathering that year. I expected a reprisal of the tougher issues that emerged around painful disagreements over how to address human sexuality. I was not disappointed.

What most captured my attention, though, was the report of the final laywoman on the panel.

"This was my first time at General Conference," she smiled. "I didn't even begin to think about it until about a week or two before I went. I arrived with an open mind."

She went on to relate her delight about the milestones celebrated: the two-hundred-fiftieth anniversary of John Street Church in New York City, the two-hundredth anniversary of Bishop Francis Asbury's death, the sixtieth anniversary of full clergy rights for women, the thirtieth anniversary of Disciple Bible Study, the upcoming twenty-fifth anniversary of Africa University and one-hundred-fiftieth anniversary of The United Methodist Women. She was amazed at all the denomination had accomplished in such a short period of time.

What a breath of fresh air to listen to her celebrate our accomplishments. For a moment, we all relaxed and rejoiced. I wonder what would happen if we insisted on these breaths of fresh air more often? If we purposefully paused and savored our successes every week? It might just energize us to carry on creatively, conscious of the positive impact we are having on the world around us, and proud of the gains we are making.

I want you to be proud of the gains you are making. And to make sure your people are in on the successes.

Another way to celebrate is to plan a large celebration. If you choose this route, draw the circle wide. Don't limit it to just the people in your congregation. Be sure to include the community at the heart of your vision. After all, they are your focus. I think about the banquet stories Jesus told where the master ordered the servants to scour the highways and byways to find guests. Add community stakeholders, neighbors, community leaders, and the rest of the faith community to the invitation list. Better yet, stage the celebration out in the community itself. When you take it off of your turf and return your focus back to the community, you definitely draw the circle wider. It's time to celebrate that what was lost has now been found. And to let people know that joy is part of the Christian life.

In the next section, I'm going to discuss three other unexpected gifts that accompany this effort. Using these gifts, you will maximize the impact of your congregation, magnify your partnership with God, and amplify your people's faith. I can't wait to share the stories of other congregations and communities around the country who are now reaping unexpected gifts because they dared to begin dreaming like Jesus.

REALIZE the Dream

Communicate and Celebrate	

Go to mydreamlikejesus.com. Download or continue completing the worksheets.
 	
Alone or with a team, write out the following:
 	
▪ **Proclaim**
  Plan three ways to communicate your good news.
 	
▪ **Celebrate the wins**
  Plan a celebration with your community. Be sure to include the who, what, where, and when.
	Communicate and Celebrate
	
	▪ _____
	
	▪ _____
	
	▪ _____
	
	▪ _____
	
	▪ _____

PART 5
Expand the Dream

*In the fourth and final step in the DARE model, **E** is for Expand. First, learn how a Jesus-like dream expands and maximizes the impact of your congregation. Second, think about how it expands and magnifies your partnership with God. Finally, enjoy how it expands and amplifies your faith, along with the faith of your people.*

CHAPTER THIRTEEN

Intensify the Impact of Your Congregation

I stood in my garden last spring, holding tiny seeds in my hand, envisioning what they would soon produce. They seemed like nothing except odd bits of earth or rock. Yet in Wyoming, tiny seeds like these shoulder through hard-packed, winter-frozen clay, unfurling tender green shoots and delicate spring flowers. No one would guess such simple, non-descript seeds could contain the makings of a whole new season. Yet, these tiny brown seeds would soon become lush rows of leafy-topped carrots. In the next bed over, purple, yellow, and green beanstalks would lift skyward, growing out of rounded seeds reminiscent of Jack and his magical beans. A few months later, my husband and I would eat as many beans and carrots as we could and give the rest away.

Jesus says tiny brown carrot seeds and unassuming beans are like the Kingdom. They grow large and are life-giving in the same way that tiny mustard seeds grow big enough for birds to perch on (Matthew 13:31-32). If a tiny seed can become like the power of the Kingdom, then consider the impact of the Kingdom-dream. Just as tiny seeds split the earth to produce vibrant new life, so declaring a visionary dream causes mountains of resignation to move and new life to animate the driest bones.

Do you know the impact your congregation is capable of making? Rev. Karen Gibson thought she knew.

"We used to do one hands-on ministry event per year," she told me. "The church would gather to distribute food to people in need. Now, because we're learning how to create a culture of renewal, we do thirty-six per year." One week per month Karen's congregation supplied and served food at the soup kitchen. A second week each month they stuffed student backpacks with peanut butter, jelly, canned fruit, pudding, and crackers so that food-insecure kids could eat over the weekend. A third week each month, the youth group met at the nursing home to lead a Wednesday night worship service. As Karen ticked off these ministries, she said, "I think that's a 50 percent increase in ministries, isn't it?"

I laughed. "Karen, you're better at ministry than you are at math. That's a 3,600 percent increase in ministries!"

"Really?" she said. "Well, we've also seen a real increase in the number of people engaged in worship too." She fed me the numbers, and we calculated the growth ... a 300 percent increase.

"Gee," she said, "That's not bad for a church with twenty people in worship." She paused for a moment. "Even though we have fewer in worship than we used to have, almost 100 percent of our worshiping congregation is engaged in hands-on ministry. We've shifted the culture of this congregation."

So, what happened to this church? How did its impact increase 3,600 percent? What made the difference? Karen came to understand that she could do more than she thought she was capable of doing. She could develop a vision and get other people on board with it. In the process, the congregation found that they could do more than they thought. Though just a small band of worshipers, together they carried out a Kingdom-sized ministry. They have intensified their congregation's impact on the community.

Rev. Steve Trout found the same thing to be true. As he and his congregation realized their dream of "A Hunger to End Hunger," they were surprised by the ripple effects that came to pass. Not only was the community of Los Alamos feeding one hundred fifty to two hundred people a month from infants to octogenarians, but a food bank from Santa Fe, forty-five miles away, also got involved. The food bank parked a semi in the church parking lot once a month to nourish eighty people.

As people lined up for the food, month after month, fall turned into winter and temperatures began to drop. The organizers noticed that the folks waiting on food had no coats. Well, that wouldn't do. The community intensified their efforts and launched a coat drive. They dignified one hundred souls with warm coats in the first season alone. The expansion of the dream was well underway. People were being fed and warmed.

That's not the only unexpected blessing that rippled out from "A Hunger to End Hunger." Greater communication and community developed among the different denominations in town. Two new churches joined Steve's church for the annual Lenten study, where Steve first cast the vision. Working together on this vision allowed pastors with very different faith commitments to see each other in a new light:

"We're different," they discovered, "not divided." From this awareness of unity, the pastors could now talk together about all kinds of issues facing the community.

In a separate dynamic, a wave of government workers retired, many of them members at Steve's church. In fact, sixty people left the church in one year. That was a big loss. The government labs, the main employer in town, searched the world for young scientists to fill the six-figure positions that became available. As a result, younger families started coming to the church. Once they come to church, they stayed because they encountered a church engaged in visible acts of love.

When's the last time you heard of scientists putting down roots in a church because the Kingdom-consciousness was so good? Well, it happened here. In fact, nuclear scientists signed up for shifts to work the food truck. A greater interchange evolved between the once isolated Ph.D. government scientists and the rest of the community. Through the act of serving and receiving food, all kinds of people came to know each other's first names. Once they didn't even know each other. Now they could call out to each other in the street or hug in the food lines.

Something else curious happened. As people ate and were satisfied, they woke up to new kinds of opportunities, and the churches woke up to new kinds of hunger. It didn't take a rocket scientist to realize that the kids of the high school educated parents were just as smart as the scientists' kids. Fully nourished, these bright kids could now concentrate enough to take Advanced Placement classes in high school, which would count for college credit. But the kids from lower income families couldn't afford to actually pay for the college credit. The church decided it would establish a scholarship to enable these kids to cover the school fees so that their hard work resulted in college credits.

"A Hunger to End Hunger" ensured that no one goes hungry in Los Alamos. But it also created a growing momentum to end other kinds of hunger. Now, there are new friendly relationships between different segments of society, new communication and unity among churches, warm coats for the winter weather, and aspiring students getting college credit.

Then came the school shooting in Parkland, Florida at the Marjorie Stoneman School. Steve was devastated. "I was just about to write an anguished newsletter article lamenting one more horrific assault when it occurred to me that I could actually do something."

It didn't take Steve long to reclaim his spiritual authority and own his agency. On a personal campaign to back up words with action, he prayed about what to do. Steve learned of a program called Guns into Gardens in which unwanted guns were bought back with grocery or gas gift cards and melted to be re-formed into garden tools. Steve and the church quickly got on board, and then invited other churches to be involved as well.

One beautiful spring morning about a month later, four pastors and thirty church folks gathered in the prayer garden on the grounds of Steve's church among the early blooms for a "swords into plowshares" experience. The morning began with a prayer walk, which highlighted the names of children who had been gunned down at school since Sandy Hook. Then guns were turned in, sawed in half on site, and prepared to be turned into garden implements. In exchange, gas and grocery cards were given out. The event wasn't huge. However, it was meaningful to take action in the face of despair.

In the midst of seemingly intractable problems like hunger, poverty, limited access to education, and lack of communal connection, one spiritual leader dared to dream like Jesus. In the process, his congregation re-discovered their purpose, connected with other churches, engaged their community, and intensified the positive impact of their congregation. I imagine these positive ripple effects will expand out for generations to come.

As you dare to dream like Jesus, and bring your dream to reality, you, too, will find that your dreams expand beyond your imagining. You are now co-creating miracles with God. Welcome to the Kingdom.

Next, let's look at how to amplify your partnership with God as you expand the dream. Turn the page to see.

EXPAND the Dream	
Count the Impacts	
Go to mydreamlikejesus.com. Download or continue completing the worksheets. Alone or with a team, write out the following: ▪ **Expected impacts** List the impacts you expected to see. ▪ **Unexpected impacts** List the impacts you didn't expect. ▪ **Intensifier element** What element intensified the impact?	**Count the Impacts** ▪ _____ ▪ _____ ▪ _____ ▪ _____ ▪ _____

CHAPTER FOURTEEN
Amplify Your Partnership with God

Rev. Dr. Eduardo (Eddie) Rivera has always been up for a challenge. Born and raised in Mexico, the son of a preacher, he followed in the footsteps of his papá and received a call to the ministry at fifteen. He took his first pulpit at eighteen. At nineteen, he learned English and at twenty-six emigrated with his young family to the United States. It is this ability to rise to a challenge that caught the attention of his bishop and elevated Eddie from pastoring one church to the responsibility of overseeing four dozen churches. In his role as district superintendent, he now supervises forty-eight United Methodist churches in the El Paso area, on the border of Mexico and Texas.

Instead of focusing on the administrative tasks at hand like ensuring that paperwork was completed on time, that meetings were conducted by the book, and that denominational offerings were paid, Eddie took a different approach. Through his participation in *Creating a Culture of Renewal*®, he dared to dream like Jesus. He developed a vision that would require all forty-eight churches in his district to operate as though they were already relevant, passionate, and life-changing by posing this question: What difference could all these congregations make to the people who lived and worked in his district?

As he posed the question, God laid this vision on his heart: "Every person within the geographical span of the El Paso District would find a place to Belong, to Believe, and to Be Useful." The sprawling El Paso District includes 1.4 million human beings. Now keep in mind that not all of these 1.4 million persons are Christian, attend church, or even care about church. And of those that do, just a small percentage are United Methodist. Yet, Eddie's vision unapologetically encompassed all 1.4 million of them.

It took guts for a denominational executive like Eddie to get beyond his own institution. It seemed counterintuitive. It might even have seemed anti-church. But it was just the opposite. Think about it. Jesus himself was on to something much bigger than refining Judaism. His dream focused on the final promise of Judaism, the final promise of God: The Kingdom of heaven. Jesus' dream encompassed Jews and Gentiles, the living and the dead, the righteous, and the not-so righteous. It was for everyone.

When you dare to dream like Jesus, you keep your eye on the big picture. You don't leave people out or focus only on your own tribe or institution. A Jesus-like dream doesn't parse small differences like ethnicity, race, gender, belief, language, sexuality, or even immigration status. A Jesus-like dream is bigger than "us versus them." It's for the whole community you find yourselves in, regardless of who lives there.

When Eddie envisioned what the El Paso region could be like once the dream was realized, he saw this: Children who didn't have a family life would be introduced to places they could belong. The de-churched, unchurched, and the "nones" would find relevant and passionate faith communities where they could believe in God and in themselves. Military person-nel stationed at Ft. Bliss would find new ways and places to be useful. Immigrants and refugees would find communi-ties that welcomed them and engender a sense of belonging. Single mothers would find places to believe again. Millenni-als would find places to channel their energies and passions, as well as ask the questions that lead to new understandings. Even temporary oil workers in the Permian Basin would find places to belong. People struggling with addictions would find places to believe that they could overcome. Couples in troubled marriages would find places to believe they have a future again. Single people would find places to step out of loneliness and isolation. The homeless would find shelter, compassion, and a fresh start.

Eddie's amazing vision contained all five surprise elements of a Jesus-like dream.

- First, it expanded assumptions about what was possible.
- Second, it was much bigger than Eddie and all forty-eight of his churches.
- Third, it had a definite fear factor to it: 1.4 million people is a lot people to reach!
- Fourth, it was about the flourishing of communities, not merely the survival of an institution.
- Fifth, it inspired people and unified them in common purpose. Not only was this vision feisty and spirited, it was downright impossible!

Eddie agrees. "Every time I bring the vision to my people, I tell them, 'This is an impossible vision. The good news is that God specializes in turning impossible dreams into possibilities.'"

Eddie organized leaders into eleven missional regions. As they met, these leaders began to ask new questions. Instead of, "I wonder who is going to show up in worship next week?" or "How will we raise enough money to get the light bill paid?" they asked themselves, "How can our congregation connect with the people in our community who want to belong, to believe, and to be useful?" This question alone upgraded their conversations, elevated their purpose, and injected new energy into their day-to-day lives. As they entertained those questions, the missional areas began to devise creative outreaches to the region. Then, one by one, with stops and starts, churches began to connect with the single mothers in their midst, the schools in their neighborhoods, and the temporary work camps out in the oilfields.

Then, the unexpected happened. The US-Mexico border exploded with waves of Central American refugees, seeking political asylum, and a safer life in the United States. Cubans and Brazilians, too, were part of this mass emigration.

All of a sudden, the vision took on new significance. How could they touch these hurting people in a way that would help them to believe, belong, and be useful? "No more business as usual," Eddie said. "We had to take bigger risks. And trust God even more." They opened up the doors of an El Paso church to provide temporary shelter for thirty to fifty refugees at a time. As their volunteer base grew more stable, they went from providing hospitality and shelter once a month to once a week. Not only that, they started to take in up to one hundred asylum-seekers at a time. Finally, the ministry became ecumenical as they partnered with a Presbyterian congregation.

Together, their hospitality made a huge difference. The refugees, traumatized from the insecurity in their homeland, the long trek through foreign countries, and inhospitable conditions in US processing centers, were given access to showers, good meals, fresh clothing, and a safe place to sleep. Volunteers at the church helped the refugees make contact with sponsors in the US, then helped them prepare to travel to where their cases would be heard in immigration court. This ministry created a way for thousands of desperate people to believe in the goodness of humanity, to experience welcome and belonging, and for a sense of usefulness to return to their spirit.

Eddie Rivera is a deeply faithful man. He took the DARE challenge. He dared to dream like Jesus, dared to align others to the dream, and dared to realize the dream. But that wasn't enough.

As he led this effort, he heard a fellow preacher quote 2 Peter 1:5-7 (NIV),

"For this very reason, make every effort to add to your faith goodness; and to goodness, knowledge; and to knowledge, self-control; and to self-control, perseverance; and to perseverance, godliness; and to godliness, mutual affection; and to mutual affection, love."

This passage convicted him. Eddie realized God was asking him to deepen his faith and their partnership once again.

"I knew the need was bigger than sheltering a hundred people a week. So, we formed a task force and approached the national office of the United Methodist Women to ask them to give us an unused community center in El Paso that had been on the market for two and a half years. We wanted to use it as a shelter." Eddie asked them if they would give it to the task force free of charge. In turn, the national office asked the task force to submit a plan of action. They did, and then waited for an answer. The answer came back. The national office said, "Yes, we're going to let you use the facilities. Free of charge. We don't even need to be involved."

Eddie and the task force took this unexpected blessing as a sign of trust. Buoyed by this seemingly miraculous turn of events, they pressed forward. Next, they requested hundreds of thousands of dollars of funding from the United Methodist Committee on Relief to refurbish the facilities. Once again, they received a yes. They hope to have the shelter completed within a few months.

This task force is not working in isolation. They have aligned their efforts with Veronica Escobar, a US Congresswoman who is leading an effort to coordinate government and non-profit responses to the flow of migrants to ease their distress.

Eddie reflected with me on how things began to unfold once he dared to dream like Jesus. "All of this gave me the guts to go beyond business as usual. It also invited me to trust God for the things I could not control. I had to trust God. If he wanted us to do this, he was going to work in the hearts of the decision-makers." Like partners in a dance, Eddie, his team, and God are co-creating miracles.

But they're not done yet. Eddie's vision continues to unfold. The next step is to establish a local branch of a national advocacy center that will bring justice for their neighbors to the south.

"I feel challenged in my faith and in my actions to be in partnership with God," Eddie said "With God's help, I am up for the challenge!" Indeed.

As you put the DARE model of dreaming like Jesus into practice, you too will find yourself responding in new and courageous ways to the spirit of God and the needs of the people around you. You will witness the positive impact of the church as you trust God in new ways.

Now that you've seen how a Jesus-like dream amplifies your partnership with God, let's turn to the third expansive quality of such a dream.

EXPAND the Dream

Praise Your Partnership

Go to mydreamlikejesus.com. Download or continue completing the worksheets.

Alone or with a team, write out the following:

- **Before**
  Note how you partnered with God before your dream.

- **After**
  Describe the growth in your partnership with God.

- **Amplifier element**
  What element amplified your partnership?

Praise Your Partnership

- _____

- _____

- _____

- _____

- _____

CHAPTER 15

Magnify Your People's Faith

"I'm tired of giving people $40 toward a shut-off notice, or a plastic grocery bag of Spam and crackers, or one night's stay in a hotel as our feeble attempt at outreach here," Rev. Tina Cross said, her voice rising with conviction. "I don't want a vision that says, 'Everyone will be fed.' It simply doesn't address the core issues here."

Tina and her husband Laird are a clergy couple whose congregation draws in people from surrounding areas. Many of the county's residents in chronic need pass through their community.

A chance conversation with a colleague, Pastor Raquel Mull, former director of the Four Corners Native American Ministry, deepened Tina's understanding of the core issues that keep her community impoverished. Raquel, a Navajo woman herself, described how difficult it was to get Navajo churches to do outreach into their own communities because of the deeply ingrained self-understanding of the people, who believe, "I have nothing; therefore, I have nothing to give." This was a pivotal moment for Tina. She realized a similarly impoverished self-understanding was at work in her community.

Co-pastors Tina and Laird were desperate to envision a way for God to transform people's whole lives by first elevating their self-identity. They thought of Paul's essential message to the church at Corinth: It doesn't matter where you start. You might not have been born into a great family, or have high status, or be well-educated. What matters is who you become in Christ. In Christ you are somebody, and you are capable of anything (1 Corinthians 1:26-29). That passage spoke to them. They would start there.

Then, as people grew in their self-understanding as capable and worthy, the congregation would equip them with the new skills needed to live successfully and abundantly: spiritually, emotionally, and physically. It would be the adage, "Give a person a fish and you feed them for a day; teach a person to fish and you feed them forever," writ large.

In developing this vision, Tina and Laird moved away from what I call a "comfort ministry" toward what I call a "challenge ministry." A comfort ministry dispenses comfort and kindness to the afflicted. It recognizes that people suffer and aims to alleviate their suffering. There's a dark side to comfort ministries, however. Offering compassion makes the giver feel good while making the receiver beholden to them; worse yet, comfort ministries can perpetuate a cycle of poverty and dependence.[41] A challenge ministry on the other hand, digs deeper to get at one or more root causes of suffering, including the person's sense of self. It addresses systemic issues and tackles larger impacts.

Up to this point, Tina and Laird's congregation had engaged in mostly comfort ministries. Frankly, comfort ministries are easier to do, quickly satisfy a need, and produce immediate results. Usually the results are not sustainable, though, because the mindset or life situation of the recipient hasn't shifted. Now, this pastoral team is going much deeper to address underlying causes and conditions.

Tina and Laird asked a new question. Instead of "How can we feed the hungry?" they asked, "Why do people go hungry in our community?" They knew that hunger itself limits the basic ability to learn, grow, relax, and move into one's highest potential. But they didn't know why it was so pervasive in their county. The answers, they discovered, involved drug addiction, alcoholism, discriminatory hiring and lending processes, and a lack of well-paying jobs. How would they address these challenges? Here's what they came up with. Their Jesus-like dream would be, "Equipping God's People to Thrive."

What I love about this vision is that it is memorable, brief, and descriptive. Yet, it still communicates the full substance and intent of the dream. Not only that, it applies equally to the people who are agents of the vision as well as the community that is the focus of it. As you'll see, this congregation is beginning to thrive in ways they couldn't imagine. You can't teach other people to recognize their inherent worth and lovability without stepping into that yourself.

As Tina found out, inspiring visions are hard to keep to yourself. Once she and Laird shared the vision with their ministry supervisor, their congregational leadership and other spiritual leaders in the community, enthusiasm spread like a lit fuse. Their vision began to call forth new resources, new people, and new participation almost immediately. "It's almost out of control!" Tina said. "At least once a month I stand up to say to the congregation, 'You won't believe what God is doing now.' God just keeps dropping stuff into our laps. Several months ago, a lady gave us a house. She happened to come to our church, heard me preach, and somehow knew she needed to give the house to us. We sold it at a discount so a young growing family could get into an affordable home. Now the family is coming to our church, too! In fact, they've become a solid part of the congregation and brought a whole new dynamic of life to this church."

This wasn't the end of Tina's tale. Next, a local bank approached them. The bank needed to reinvest in the community as they had a large donation fund that needed to be used. The bank chose their church's college scholarship fund to invest in. It used to be that Tina and Laird's church granted one hundred scholarships of $300 each. This year, after the bank blessed them, they were able to give away one hundred fifty scholarships of $800 each. That's almost triple the amount given to half again as many students.

Tina had one more miracle story to share with me. A well-respected charter school approached them, looking for a new location. "They looked at our gargantuan building and said, 'We'd like to lease and build the entire upstairs.'" It's not a done deal, Tina cautioned, but it's looking good. If the school moves in, that will help this congregation sustain itself for years to come.

Do you get the picture? Tina and Laird stopped settling for ministry as normal, worked up the courage to dream like Jesus, began to share that vision with others, and now the universe is aligning with the dream. So is the congregation itself. People who used to come for handouts now receive conversation, counseling, and options they never had before. One young family, one hundred fifty students, and potentially an entire school is also being equipped to thrive. "God trusts us to be stewards of these possibilities because of our vision: 'To equip people to thrive.' As a result, we are being entrusted with even bigger responsibilities."

As you can imagine, the vision and the miraculous string of events it generated has had quite an impact on the church. Take Stella Martinez. She's the Communications Coordinator on staff. "Once we developed this vision to equip people to thrive," she said, "I felt called that I needed to change my life so that I could help others change theirs." Stella retired from a twenty-five-year teaching career so that she could devote everything she knew to the ministry of the church. "Now, everything I see, I look at through the lens of the church's vision to equip people to thrive." She realized she could be part of the vision in her own way. This dream has magnified her faith in beautiful ways.

Stella and her husband Jaime love to drive up to a nearby mountain town. There they spotted a beautiful street-side community cupboard that says, "Take what you need, leave what you can." It's filled with non-perishable goods. This made an impression on her. Back at work, she began thinking about building one in her town. Then she saw a man digging through the dumpster by the church. "Why isn't he coming in?" she wondered. "Surely he would know that we could give him food." Pride and shame, she imagined, kept him from doing so. It was one more impetus for Jaime and Stella to build a street-side community cupboard and erect it on the corner by the church.

One day a woman came into the church for a bus token. She leaned in and confided, "I really need some feminine products." The church didn't have any. Now Stella is making sure they are stocked in the box as well. "Just being here, knowing where we want to go, opens my eyes to things like that. Something as small as that would have done a lot for this woman."

Do you get the picture? A Jesus-like dream expands the faith of everyone it touches. Now let's dive a little deeper and see how this works. Jesus affirmed that the Kingdom is within. In the same way, a Jesus-like dream affirms the wholeness of each person. It encourages you to discover the goodness that is already with you. Then it empowers you to embrace that goodness and act on it.

There are two important implications here for faith expansion. First, your own faith in yourself expands as you recognize the sacred goodness within you. Second, other people's faith will expands as they recognize that same inherent goodness within them. Thus, your ministries engender freedom not dependency; they empower not shackle. Your efforts call forth the humanity of others rather than assume some innate deficiency.

If the Kingdom of God is within, that means the people or creatures you aim to serve already possess the same radiant divine spark within them as you yourself do. They may be unaware of it. If that's the case, the issue is not to save them but to awaken them to who and what is already within them. Your ministry becomes the pathway to fully accessing and expressing the divine love and power that already resides within them. In Wesleyan theology, that power is called "prevenient grace." Matthew Fox terms it "original blessing." Your joyous task is to empower others to tap into the divine guidance that resides within in order to access the inherent goodness, desire, intelligence, love, and wisdom all their own.

Visions are most life-giving when you connect people to their own internal knowledge of God and Kingdom. As much as people sometimes protest, most folks generally don't want to be fixed or saved. It requires them to be a victim, stripped of their dignity, and robbed of their own sense of self. Your job is not to diminish those God-given qualities in a single soul, but to enhance them and enable others to step up into their own Kingdom inheritance. The Biblical vision of community is people who come together to manifest the Kingdom in the here and now.

Recently, I had the opportunity to hear Ed Wingfield, a one-time Executive Director of the former Colorado Black Chamber of Commerce Foundation, speak on leadership. Like many leadership organizations, they aimed to equip and inspire the next generation of leadership. "Using current models of leadership, a few heroes rise economically in the community, but no one else advances. If we're not careful," he warned, "organizations like ours could unintentionally reinforce victimhood, then set out to rescue folks from it."

As I listened to him speak, I realized his was a familiar story. We in the church fall into that trap, too. We have something to give therefore others must receive from us. We say we want to level the playing field, to help the "underprivileged" but instead we perpetually tip it. Leveling the playing field comes from empowering others to tap into their own abilities. Chesie Lee, a woman I coached through *Creating a Culture of Renewal*® sought to transform this dynamic in the church's relationship to Native Americans. I knew what she meant. I had been on several mission trips to Rosebud Indian Reservation, home of the Lakota Sioux in South Dakota. We would paint homes, do minor repairs, and in the evening learn about history and customs. We were excited to paint homes and make a difference for "underprivileged" people. I didn't know how our efforts actually came across until Chesie told me that a common response to the question, "Who wants to have their house painted this year?" is typically, "Nah, I've had mine painted three years in a row." In other words, we weren't really meeting needs.

Chesie had her pulse on a truer need and wanted to launch a new conversation. At the time, she was the executive director of the Wyoming Association of Churches. As she dared to dream like Jesus, she co-facilitated the creation of the Wind River Native Advocacy Center together with members of the Northern Arapaho and Eastern Shoshone tribes. The Center was founded on the premise that Native Americans are most "helped" when they are empowered to advocate for themselves, such as at the State Legislature. Not the old model of painting houses that didn't really need painting. Instead of organizing home repair trips to the Wind River Reservation, which kept the Northern Arapaho and Eastern Shoshone in the victim role of "lesser than," Chesie invited church groups to come to the reservation to learn from the tribes. This way, instead of being pigeonholed as "underprivileged" people to be rescued, the Native Americans, and their inherent agency, would be acknowledged. They would be affirmed as human beings with valuable wisdom to offer others. Chesie envisioned these mission trips as an opportunity for mutual education and upliftment.

Turns out this was a tough vision to communicate. Many churches resisted the idea that coming to receive would be as worthwhile as coming to give. The few who did come discovered something of a new connectedness and a different view of history. They discovered something of the Kingdom within.

In Acts 2:42-47 (NIV), we have a sense of people enjoying salvation or wholeness, sharing what they have. This is different than the greater rescuing the lesser.

They devoted themselves to the apostles' teaching and to fellowship, to the breaking of bread and to prayer. Everyone was filled with awe at the many wonders and signs performed by the apostles. All the believers were together and had everything in common. They sold property and possessions to give to anyone who had need. Every day they continued to meet together in the temple courts. They broke bread in their homes and ate together with glad and sincere hearts, praising God and enjoying the favor of all the people. And the Lord added to their number daily those who were being saved.

So, a Jesus-like dream is something that dignifies the individual as well as the community. Like sanctification, in which an inward change of the soul works its way outward into visible expression, causing a ripple of blessedness all around them, a Jesus-like dream begins as a spark of imagination, which permeates and uplifts the consciousness, then flows outward into reality calling a new state of affairs into being.

Now that you have discovered the three ways a Jesus-like dream is expanded, it's time to turn our attention the future.

EXPAND the Dream	
Delight in Faith	
Go to mydreamlikejesus.com. Download or continue completing the worksheets. Alone or with a team, write out the following: - **Pre-dream faith** Identify how you and your people related to God. - **Living-the-dream faith** Describe how you and your people's faith has grown. - **Magnifying element** What element magnified their faith? What element magnified your faith?	**Delight in Faith** ▪ _____ ▪ _____ ▪ _____ ▪ _____ ▪ _____

CHAPTER SIXTEEN

Foster New Dreams

Our lives are built on the dreams of others. For example, my grandmother, Miriam Goldberg, recently died at the age of one hundred. She was old and full of years, as the Scriptures say. Her passing has occasioned the telling of many stories about how she and my grandfather Max lived in their early years of marriage. She was raised a Reform Jew, and he was raised in a traditional Jewish way, making him what we today would call an Orthodox Jew. In 1936, that kind of marriage was risky and innovative. It foreshadowed the kind of creative energies that were married in their union. They were also dreamers. Miriam dreamed of a house full of children. Max dreamed of harnessing new technology. While she raised their four children (including my mother Dorothy), Max launched a radio show, a talk show, and a man on the street column. He also brought the first TV station to Denver.

But they lived in Denver at a time when anti-Semitism was a hard, discriminating reality. My mother felt it directly. She was one of a few Jewish kids in her class. Other kids taunted her as she got on the Hebrew School bus after school. The community had even larger troubles including the fact that Jewish doctors were not welcomed in any of the hospitals. Max and Miriam envisioned a Denver where the Jewish community could survive and thrive. After World War II, they raised money to establish a hospital where Jewish doctors could practice their calling. It was named Rose Hospital, for a Jewish World War II hero. They also shepherded a fledgling weekly newspaper that would hold together the growing Jewish community of the Queen City of the Plains, the Intermountain Jewish News. When Max died of cancer at the age of sixty-one, my grandmother stepped into his shoes and led the newspaper through great spurts of growth and development for the next thirty-five years. She finally laid down her red wax editing pencil for the final time in her nineties. My mother caught the writing bug from her parents and carried on their love of family and Judaism.

At the same time that my Mom was growing up in Denver, and was the first of two girls in the city to have a *Bat Mitzvah* (a Jewish coming of age ceremony normally reserved for boys at that time in history), my Dad was growing up in rural Connecticut in an Italian and Polish household of immigrants and entrepreneurs. My father followed in his own father's footsteps and became a successful entrepreneur, starting his first business when he was in eighth grade. My father continued to be self-employed through high school, then college, where he met my mother. Over time, my parents built a successful business that employed over one hundred fifty people.

In my generation, four of the five siblings have caught the entrepreneurial bug, each running our own businesses doing what we love. Two of us are also writers. In a sense, each of us is building on the dreams of our parents and grandparents.

154

One dream begets another and opens up the doorway to still more possibilities. In the same way, the whole Christian movement is built on Jesus' dream, first uttered two thousand years ago. While it's been stultified through institution-building, power consolidation, and periods of misguided and even violent attempts to coerce others into faith, at the heart of it is still, "Thy Kingdom come, thy will be done, on earth as it is in heaven."

As leaders dare to dream like Jesus, their dreams expand deep into communities, inspiring even more dreams.

Kerry Wood, for example, is the thirty-something pastor of a once large, bustling church. It used to be a leading presence in her small city. But over thirty years, the congregation declined in both membership and influence. It stagnated under overwhelming financial difficulties. Plagued by a sense of despair, the congregation witnessed its options for the future receding. Through her participation in *Creating a Culture of Renewal®,* Kerry proactively stepped into her authority as a bold leader, newly certain that the extraordinary is possible when God is present. First, she reclaimed her authority, owned her agency, and dared to dream like Jesus.

Next, she started to prepare the soil for a different kind of message. No more "same old same old." That wouldn't change anything in this congregation. Knowing that the adults were listening to the children's message as intently as the children were, she began to insert playful and bold aspects of the Gospel into her brief messages, inspiring the whole congregation to become more playful and willing to take risks. After planting these seeds, Kerry began to learn what the congregation valued, what inspired them, and what made them anxious. She dove into understanding her congregational culture and intentionally established ministry teams with a balance of archetypes. Then, she began to capitalize on her gifts, pinpoint her fears, and take ground in demonstrating more effective leadership behaviors. "It was eye-opening for me to realize that church conflicts get out of hand because I

155

don't take the issues as seriously as those involved do," Kerry reported. "I adopted a strategy of checking in with a trusted lay leader about the seriousness of conflicts. I learned how to test my assumptions, ask pertinent questions, and be ready to hear peoples' answers. This has empowered us all to deal with conflicts early and effectively."

Finally, Kerry turned to receiving, clarifying, and communicating an inspiring vision. Her vision was to establish a group of followers of Jesus—people who already consider themselves disciples—to intentionally take the next step of faith and develop themselves into a community of apostles. They would take personal responsibility for leading like Jesus.

As she gained alignment for this vision, Kerry could tell something was different. Instead of just giving a perfunctory "yes" to the vision, the congregation came forward with concrete ways to be involved. "Together, we established a covenant community in which we would grow as apostles," Kerry told me, excitement in her voice. "I had hoped to begin with twelve people and increase to twenty-four by the end of the year. Instead we started with eighteen!"

No wonder she was excited. Kerry's vision was countering the eight symptoms of decline, one by one. Her group established a weekly prayer group which became the fertile soil out of which the new covenant community began to grow, ready to be sent by Jesus beyond the walls of the church.

As if a group of eighteen apostles who are growing in spiritual depth isn't enough, other visions unfolded under Kerry's expanding skill as a leader. "We now have a Garden Giveaway," Kerry related to me, "where local gardeners share the abundance of their gardens with the people on fixed incomes in our community."

In addition to adding two raised beds and container gardens on the church property, the Garden Giveaway program is led by a visioning team of seven people. The

Garden Giveaway gained such momentum that it attracted interest from city officials and land trust managers which in turn led to an invitation for Kerry to be a panelist at a state-wide land trust conference. Not only that, it inspired a benefit concert and opened the possibility of taking over a vacant lot in the city center for a community garden program. Do you see what happened here? Daring to dream like Jesus inspired others to do the same. Wow!

While some pundits speak of a "death tsunami" in the United Methodist Church, Kerry and her people experienced the opposite: a life-giving cascade of Jesus-like dreams which nurtured every area of church life. For one, worship was enlivened. That year, eighteen new people participated in executing worship at the church by writing original music and dramas, planting gardens, contributing artwork and crafts to worship, incorporating sign language into worship, and creating sensory experiences of scripture.

Missions too, was buoyed. The Missions Committee began offering mission "on-ramps." These simple monthly mission opportunities included activities such as donating supplies to the homeless shelter and food bank, making clothing for children, and raising a scholarship for a community arts program.

The momentum didn't end there. Next, the church began working toward two other visions: to restructure under a simplified board model and to become a reconciling congregation, openly accepting people from the gay, lesbian, and trans-gendered community into the life of the church.

Although Kerry instigated these expansions, others in the church have stepped forward to take leadership of them. That's how apostolic leadership works: one leader empowers others, just like Jesus did.

"Before working with you, Rebekah," Kerry told me, "I supported 'doable' visions in the churches I served. Now, I've learned how to dream like Jesus, and I've taught my congregation how to do so, too. Dreaming like Jesus," Kerry said, "has helped me to embrace adventure and to trust that with God all things are possible. I understand God as limitless in a way that I never have before."

Kerry's story is inspiring. But it's not unique. Once you have begun to dream like Jesus, to tap into his magnificent vision of an earth that reflects heaven, you'll find that it's hard to stop! You have now tapped into the flow of vision, where you are deeply connected with the source of dreams. You'll know that nothing is truly impossible. You'll know without a shadow of a doubt that the age of miracles is not over, and that you have entered the realm of intentional co-creation with God. Now, do you dare to step into Jesus' next dream for you?

CHAPTER SEVENTEEN

Jesus' Next Big Dream for the World

As inspiring as they are, our dreams pale in comparison to Jesus' next big dream for us: accepting the mantle of apostleship.

What's the difference between a "disciple" and an "apostle?" The word disciple comes from the Latin *discipulus,* meaning scholar. A disciple is a student of Jesus' whose primary focus in on mastering his teachings so that he or she can live out Jesus' way.

An apostle, however, has a different focus. The word apostle derives from the Greek *apostolos* meaning envoy. While disciples are students, apostles are proactive agents, who act on behalf of the one who has sent them. In today's language, we might say that disciples are followers and apostles are leaders. But there's more to it.

The biggest difference between disciples and apostles is that apostles possess a qualitatively different kind of faith than disciples. Disciples have faith in Jesus. Apostles, on the other hand, have the faith of Jesus. Otherwise, there's no way apostles could do what Jesus did.

When the twelve functioned as disciples, they followed and learned from Jesus, asking him many questions. However, when they functioned as apostles, they walked on water, multiplied loaves and fish, healed the sick, and oversaw the multiplication of the church. Disciples ask WWJD? Apostles answer this question by stepping up into courageous faith and miracle-making action.

As I write this, the United States is experiencing a retrogressive wave of hate rallies, fueled by fear of the other and inflamed by divisive rhetoric. Neo-Nazi rallies and Ku Klux Klan gatherings signal that something many of us thought had died had simply been buried. At the same time, public shootings are becoming increasingly common. Not even churches, synagogues, hospitals, or yoga studios are off-limits. These bursts of hate-mongering and violence are deeply troubling.

Where is the Kingdom dream in the midst of this?

Countless congregations are themselves polarized by politics, hamstrung by conflicting loyalties, and lined up behind political leaders – however glaring their shortcomings – rather than Jesus' own teachings. Congregations have confused the visions of political leaders and their fight for power with the Kingdom vision of Jesus, their own chief visionary. This capacity to be easily fractured points to a conspicuous lack of a unifying vision. Both in our country and in our churches. When it comes to churches, I'm not suggesting that Christians in America abandon democratic ideals or revert to some sort of authoritarian theocracy. However, I am suggesting that we must let Kingdom-based ethics shape our politics rather than the other way around.

The time for apostleship is now. As the world grows more complex, and the rate of change speeds up, it's easy to sit back, overwhelmed by the enormity of problems. Mass shootings are becoming a new norm. Police violence against young black men and women has emerged from the hazy shadows into the unblinking lens of video cameras. Democratic institutions are being undermined by a culture of bullying and dishonesty, where wielding power over others is more

160

important than sharing power with others. Honesty and truthfulness, civility and inclusion, justice, and fairness – aspirational principles that have long guided democracy – are threatened, replaced by autocratic and corrupt impulses. This is true not only in the United States, but around the world.

Undocumented children have been forcibly separated from their parents, abetted by exploitive interpretations of the Bible. They are locked up behind bars in filthy, overcrowded detention centers that belie human decency.[42] False equivalencies have been drawn between white supremacists and civil rights protesters. Growing anti-Semitism, anti-Muslim, anti-Christian, and anti-immigrant sentiments are expanding around the globe. This loss of social civility, democratic norms, and cultural sensitivity to those who are different from the mainstream may take years, even generations, to overcome. Previously, those of us who rejoiced at our national progress shown by electing a biracial US president and affirming marriage equality for all people, have been stunned at the subsequent rise of an authoritarian president on this same soil, a man who governs through intimidation, bullying, and truth-twisting tweets.

Where is the Kingdom, we wonder? Yet, Jesus whispers then, as now, the Kingdom is within. It's near. It's at hand.

We are being called to live such that we manifest the Kingdom in ways small and large. If the Kingdom of God can't be lived out in this world as it is, it can't be lived out. We are to practice evoking the divine impulse within right here, right now on this earth, with all its messiness, contradictions, chaos, competing stories and conflicting worldviews. Earth is where we are meant to imprint the love and light of heaven.

Indeed, even as the world grows more complex and divided, and even as we are on the verge of seeming collapse, we are also at the threshold of unprecedented transformation.

At the national level, for example, more women and young

people than ever before are running for public office. Students who witnessed their classmates being shot have taken to the halls of congress and to TV cameras, eloquently and unequivocally calling for a moratorium on gun violence. Brave elected officials have begun to interrupt partisan silence, elevating truth over falsehood. Courageous women have chosen to risk all by speaking up and claiming the sanctity of their own experience, lives, and bodies. Coalitions of black, white, gay, and straight people have gathered to say that black and brown lives matter as much as white and blue lives.

This chorus of courageous voices demands of us that we not only dream like Jesus, but that we believe like Jesus. That we not only have faith in Jesus but demonstrate the faith of Jesus in our own lives. It's time to step out of what we think is possible into what we have believed is impossible. Life is not a fixed reality. Today's actions do not determine tomorrow's possibilities. There is far more goodness, creative power, and divinity within each of us than we have yet tapped. "With God, all things are possible."

Why sit back and wait for something to happen to you when you can be an agent of life? This is the time for churches to speak up and to reiterate Jesus' dream of the reign and realm of God. God's own power flows through you. You are an empowered being of love and light. You are a spiritual being having a human experience. Like Jesus, you, too, have the power to create worlds with your words and to shift entire realities. You are now in a position to fulfill the dreams of Jesus. As a steward of the Gospel dream, this is your primary responsibility.

While the Kingdom dream is decidedly earthy and this-worldly, there's a spiritual aspect to it as well. It addresses an internal wholeness, an expanded consciousness, an awakening to the divine presence within. Not just within Jesus, but within all of us.

Created in the image and likeness of God, you bear the

divine imprint of blessing, creativity, and imagination in every cell of your body. The very being-ness of God dwells within you. You are designed in such a way that your thoughts become things. Your word has the power to re-orient the shape and flow of circumstances. You are a quantum being clothed in a body made of stardust and spirit. Your every prayer receives God's abundant answer. Amazing, isn't it? If only you saw yourself this way every day.

What might life be like if you saw yourself through God's eyes? What might life be like if you knew, with every cell of your being, that you were wholly beloved, a bearer of divine light, made perfect in weakness, called and appointed for such a time as this? How might your congregation function if you and they knew there was nothing to fear? What about your community?

It's time to take the next step into this new mindset, this new consciousness. Let me suggest a powerful step in this direction. Reframe your petitions into answered prayers. In other words, pray as though you know that your prayers have already been answered. Praying with the end in mind alerts you to your co-creative powers, the twinning of your humanity and divinity. Moreover, it also deepens your trust in Jesus' promise that he will do anything you ask in his name. That whatever you seek you will find, and that no door remains closed to you.

Start by praying Jesus' dream from this perspective. Instead of "Our father who art in heaven, hallowed be thy name, Thy Kingdom come thy will be done, on earth as it is in heaven" try this: "God, we thank you that your Kingdom is here, that your will is being done, and that even now, earth reflects the abundance of heaven."

Or even better yet, try this: "God we are so grateful that your Kingdom has come, that it is within us, around us, and very near to us. We thank you that we have done your will. We thank you that earth now reflects something of heaven. That we have dreamed your dreams, that we have fulfilled the promise, that your dream has become reality. We thank you that you have given us our daily bread, that you have led us away from temptation, and delivered us from evil. We thank you that you have shared your Kingdom, power, and glory with us for ever and ever! Amen!"

Presumptuous, you say? No. Repeatedly, Jesus tells you your prayers are answered. Now is the time to live with that confidence. Praying as though your prayers have already been answered, and thanking God in advance, moves you firmly from this dream to the next, from disciple to apostle. All while giving you the courage to match your increased faith with grander actions.

Who you know yourself to be is a mere glimmer of what you are about to become. Jesus speaks of your ability to move mountains with your faith, of your ability to heal as he healed. He even speaks of you surpassing his works. It all starts with your own perspective. Perspective shapes reality. For all intents and purposes, perspective is reality. What you believe you can achieve. What you don't believe, well, you won't.

Now that you have glimpsed the future, it's time to wrap up the process. In the next chapter, we'll bring it all together.

CHAPTER EIGHTEEN
Conclusion

George Bullard's pivotal work, *The Life Cycle and Stages of a Congregation,* reinforces what the author of Proverbs once said, "Without a vision the people perish" (Proverbs 29:18, KJV). Turns out this proverb holds true for churches, too. Bullard demonstrates that congregational vitality hinges on one key dynamic: the maintenance and re-invention of a vitalizing vision. Programs, people, and proper management aren't enough. Even money isn't enough. Without a vision, not only do people perish, but so do churches.

I have found in the work I do with churches around the country that the vast majority of ministries are inward focused, strictly designed to comfort us. Maybe one-fourth of our ministries are outward focused and designed to challenge us and bless others. I fear that American Christianity has stopped daring greatly and switched to cruise control. Cruise control is great, as long as it works. But in older models of cars, as in older congregations, cruise control is not known for its durability.

I used to drive a 1995 Toyota Rav4. I loved the way it looked, felt, and drove. That is, until the cruise control stopped working. In those days, the legal speed limit in Wyoming was seventy miles per hour. I would set my speed for seventy-two, cruising paved-over prairies lined with sagebrush under the shadow of rising mountain peaks.

Before long, my speed of seventy-two gave way to seventy, then slipped down to sixty-five miles per hour. It was hard to tell when the cruise control first disengaged. I would think I was maintaining my speed until other vehicles appeared on the lonely highway and passed me. The same is true in older congregations. You can't stay in aging cruise control long without losing momentum. Before you know it, you've slowed down to a crawl and it's all about survival.

The survival mode isn't working for most of your congregations. Between the "none's" (those who claim no religious affiliation, making up about 23 percent of the US population),[43] and the "dones" (those who once claimed religious affiliation but are now done with organized religion and who make up about approximately 20 percent of the US population), the rolls of the church's alumni are growing faster than the rolls of active membership. Add to that the "spiritual but not religious" (those who are connected to God or a Higher Power but not through church and who make up 27 percent of the US population), and there are more people not going to church than are.

Even pastors and leaders are burned out. Tired of the fighting, stagnation, and resistance to the change they encounter in the congregations they lead, and in the denominations themselves, pastors leave the church well before retirement. They feel discouraged, depressed, and guilty about not fulfilling their call to serve effectively. This is especially true of young pastors and female clergy. They burn out at a faster rate than older male clergy. No matter who burns out, though, everyone loses when spiritual leaders and the people they serve – all of whom claim to follow Jesus – neglect to tap into the power of Jesus' own dream.

I can relate. Every time I've gotten discouraged enough to consider walking away from the people who gather in his name, or from the religious community that honors him, my own waking vision of Jesus from thirty years ago reminds me that he was intentional about coming to me. Out of that profound encounter, I've developed a Jesus-like dream, that I have shared in a previous chapter, which guides my ministry. That's the power of vision. It calls you back. It reminds you why you do what you do.

When you operate without vision, the real casualty is the community you serve. When you refuse to exercise your right to dream like Jesus, when you forget to love your neighbors as yourselves, when survival becomes more important than service, the community you serve becomes spiritually impoverished. Your lack of engagement reinforces a corresponding lack of interest from the community in joining you. Bottom line: leaders and their congregations are simply going through the motions of doing church rather than being church, of stewarding budgets and buildings rather than the dreams of Jesus.

As challenging as all this is, there is good news. Take, for example, the situation Rev. Madeleine Tyler found herself in when she was appointed to Spruce Mountain Church in the foothills of North Carolina. Shortly after she arrived at the church, she enrolled into my program, *Creating a Culture of Renewal*®. Her new church had been embroiled in conflict. The previous pastor had been moved in a hurry. It wasn't a large church to begin with. When two-thirds of the worshipers left in the wake of the conflict, it shrunk considerably. The remnant felt aggrieved about the sudden changes in their previously stable congregation. Too loyal and dutiful to leave, though, they avoided making any further decisions, afraid of stirring up more conflict.

In the meantime, Spruce Mountain Church's fear of disturbing the status quo translated into a string of missed opportunities for ministry. Worship attendance had plummeted. Giving followed suit. Spruce Mountain Church's communal prayers followed the expected pattern of prayer for churches in survival mode: personal health, safe travels, and comfort for those who had experienced a death in the family. Not very many people were involved in ministries. Bottom line: not much was happening at this church. In fact, as Madeleine got to know the congregation, it became apparent that not much had happened at this church despite the efforts of the previous pastor either. Clearly, this was a church without a guiding vision or a Jesus-like dream.

Once Madeleine arrived and surveyed the situation, she took what she was learning from *Creating a Culture of Renewal*® and applied it. First, she dealt with two of the most obvious symptoms of decline: problem people and dead-end decision-making. She helped the church members re-frame the conflict they had weathered and to see their differences in a positive light. Second, she led them through a process to establish a relational covenant with one another. They agreed upon rules of civil engagement, including how to disagree and dissent. These clear-cut, yet gracious boundaries solidified a sense of safety for all while giving a voice to the disenchanted.

With those guidelines in place, she was next able to address sluggish giving. Spruce Mountain Church took on its first stewardship campaign in fifteen years. Nine out of every ten people participated, and almost 100 percent of the budget was pledged by the end of the six-week campaign. Building on this strong foundation, new hope flowed back into the congregation. Worship attendance rebounded. Visitors not only came, they returned and became active in the church. As worship grew stronger, Madeleine concentrated on vigorous prayer for a vision.

At the same time, she took on Spruce Mountain Church's insulated focus. Many young families had left during the conflicted time of the church and when they did, many of the hands-on ministries disappeared, too. It became clear that the younger families' involvement had masked the insulated focus of the church. In working towards God's promising future, Madeleine realized that they needed to look outward. That's when she saw an opening. As the congregation continued to pray for guidance to be a healthy, whole church again, her discernment led to the vision that she began to cast, "Building community with our neighbors to better serve Jesus together."

To her great credit, Madeleine didn't try to do this work herself. Instead, she raised up a new set of leaders to help carry out the vision. These new leaders organized a Senior Vacation Bible School to connect with the aging, unchurched population around them. Children's Vacation Bible School came next, a real leap of faith since only five kids currently attended the church. The leadership team also realized no fresh or nutritious food was available within six miles of most of the community. Spruce Mountain Church was situated in the middle of a food desert. They began to offer a free, nutritional Sunday morning breakfast. Unfortunately, the breakfast didn't reach the intended population. Still hopeful, the leadership hasn't given up yet.

"We're perceived as a white church," Madeleine reflected, "where non-white people aren't welcome. Since 51 percent of our neighbors aren't white, we're actively working on building trust."

Spruce Mountain Church started a "Loads of Love Laundromat Ministry" and a house church, both promising ways to meet new people and connect with new families.

If the leaders of this church are successful, the relationships they are building will reflect Jesus' dream of heaven on earth. Whether they gather in the sanctuary, the laundromat, the house church, the soccer field, or the diner, their congregation has begun to mirror the ethnic makeup and concerns of their neighbors.

Like Madeleine, you, too, can learn how to dream like Jesus. You can learn how to envision and co-create new futures with God once more. I have seen clergy and lay leaders around the country—in congregations large and small, urban and rural—step into their spiritual authority, reclaim Jesus' power to dream, and co-create miracles with God and their congregations. They have learned how to speak new realities into being. Friends, there are success stories all over the country. Let's make one for your church.

You don't have to wait for some better time, better place, better people, or for heaven or judgment day. All that you need is now within your grasp. There is no "there" to get to first. There is no need to procrastinate or perfect yourself. The time is now. God's love is now. God's power is now. It's time to dream like Jesus.

Resources for Renewal

Rebekah and her team offer a wide range of workshops, programs, and coaching services for church leaders and congregations seeking renewal. For more information on the resources listed below, visit: www.rebekahsimonpeter.com.

FREE RESOURCES:

Access Rebekah's weekly blogs for *Creating a Culture of Renewal*®. Also watch for new videos and articles.

WORKSHOPS:

Speed up the process of renewal while reducing resistance to change with *The Platinum Rule for Thriving Congregations*. Upgrade your leadership culture as you move *From Discipleship to Apostleship*. Discover miracle-making power as you *Lead Like Jesus*. Build bridges of understanding with *Productive Conflict*.

Dream Like Jesus®

Deepen your faith and bring the impossible to life through the **Dream Like Jesus® Leadership Academy**, an exciting eighteen-month congregational journey through the DARE model.

www.dreamlikejesus.com

Creating a Culture of Renewal®

Through three nine-month tracks, denominational leaders, clergy and lay leaders are empowered to:

- Craft a bold vision that exponentially expands what you and your congregation thought possible.
- Dramatically increase the number of people actively engaged in ministry.
- Transform a risk-averse culture into a congregation willing to dream like Jesus, enthusiastically tackling new initiatives and launching new ministries.

CONFERENCES AND WORKSHOPS:

Rebekah speaks at conferences, convocations, and retreats, and conducts specialized workshops for denominational leaders. Visit:

www.rebekahsimonpeter.com

to request her to speak at your event.

INDIVDUAL COACHING: Rebekah offers individual coaching for leaders who are ready to move beyond limited thinking and predictable results to transform their personal and professional lives.

For more information about these resources
and services, visit:

www.rebekahsimonpeter.com

Notes

1   There are 152 references to the Kingdom in the New Testament alone.

2   Bourgeault, Cynthia. *The Wisdom Jesus: Transforming Heart and Mind, A New Perspective on Christ and His Message,* Shambhala, 2008.

3   Rohr, Richard. *The Universal Christ: How a Forgotten Reality Can Change Everything We See, Hope For, and Believe,* Convergent Books, 2019.

4   Sanford, Johan. *The Kingdom Within: The Inner Meaning of Jesus' Sayings,* HarperOne, 2009.

5   O'Murchu, Diarmuid. *Quantum Theology: Spiritual Implications of the New Physics,* Crossroad Publishing, 2004.

6   Levine, Amy-Jill. *Short Stories by Jesus: The Enigmatic Parables of a Controversial Rabbi,* HarperOne, 2015.

7   Matthew is the only Gospel that uses the term Kingdom of heaven, rather than Kingdom of God. The term can be found in the following twenty-two verses: Matthew 3:2, 4:17, 5:3, 5:10, 5:19, 5:20, 7:21, 8:11, 10:7, 11:11, 11:12, 13:11, 13:44, 13:45, 13:47, 13:52, 16:19, 18:1, 18:3, 18:4, 18:23, and 19:12.

8   Exodus 20:6 in Jewish Bibles and Exodus 20:7 in Christian Bibles.

9   See Exodus 20:7. As a point of interest, both Jews and Protestants number this commandment as the third of ten commandments. In the Catholic canon, however, this commandment is counted as the second out of ten.

10   Hannam, James. *The Genesis of Science; How the Christian Middle Ages Launched the Scientific Revolution.* Washington, DC: Regnery Publishing, 2011.

11   Feld, Marlin. "SUMMARY OF WESTERN CLASSICAL MUSIC HISTORY." Columbia University. Accessed December 29, 2018. http://www.columbia.edu/itc/music/ito/history/.

12   Simon-Peter, Rebekah, *The Jew Named Jesus: Discover the Man and His Message,* Abingdon Press, 2013.

13   Grant, Tobin. "The Great Decline: 60 years of religion in one graph." ReligionNews.com. January 27, 2014. https://religionnews.com/2014/01/27/great-decline-religion-united-states-one-graph/

14   Numbers vary on the state of the Roman Catholic church. While the Vatican says the Catholic population is growing exponentially, other trusted religious research organizations come up with different numbers, especially for US Catholics.

Frazer, Kelly. "Is the Catholic Church Experiencing Exponential Growth or Declining?" World Religion News. Accessed April 28, 2019.https://www.worldreligionnews.com/religion-news/is-the-catholic-church-experiencing-exponential-growth-or-declining.

Meanwhile, growth in the Latter-Day Saints or Mormon population has slowed to less than 1.5%, its lowest reported rate of growth since 1937.

Religion News Service. "Mormon growth continues to slow, especially in the US." Accessed June 17, 2018. https://religionnews.com/2018/04/13/mormon-growth-continues-to-slow-especially-in-the-u-s/

15   Jones, Jeffrey. "U.S. Church Membership Down Sharply in Past Two Decades." April 18, 2019. https://news.gallup.com/poll/248837/church-membership-down-sharply-past-two-decades.aspx.

16   These ideas are most notably explored in *The Great Emergence* by Phyllis Tickle in her 2008 volume and *Christianity after Religion* by Diana Butler Bass in her 2013 volume.

17   Thomas Friedman's 2008 book Hot, Flat and Crowded, describes the convergence of three intersecting dynamics: global warming, globalization and population growth.

18   Farrar, Straus and Giroux. *God In Search of Man: A Philosophy of Judaism*, 1976.

19   Paulikas, Steven. "Mayor Pete and the Queering of the American Soul." April 17, 2019.https:// www.nytimes.com/2019/04/17/opinion/mayor-pete-and-the-queering-of-the-american-soul.html?-searchResultPosition=7.

20   George Bullard's helpful work on the life cycle of a congregation highlights how vision is the most telling barometer of the health of churches today.

21   A *targum* is a paraphrase or explanation of a sacred Jewish text. *Targumim* (plural) date from the century prior to the birth of Christ. Binding and loosing appears in Matthew 16:19.

22   Here's the quote from Matthew 23:23. It's strikingly relevant to the church today. "Woe to you, teachers of the law and Pharisees, you hypocrites! You give a tenth of your spices–mint, dill and cumin. But you have neglected the more important matters of the law–justice, mercy and faithfulness. You should have practiced the latter, without neglecting the former."

23   According to Kevin Dunn, the current Director of Data Services of the General Council on Finance and Administration, baptisms in The United Methodist Church in the US no longer keep pace with burials. While both have been on a downward trend as membership overall has declined, the number of baptisms fell below the number of people removed from church rolls in 2011. A slight uptick in baptisms performed in 2012 seemed hopeful. But the number slid dramatically in 2012 and every year thereafter.

As of 2017, baptisms in Southern Baptist churches were at a seventy-year low. Shellnutt, Kate. "Hundreds of New Churches Not Enough to Satisfy Southern Baptists." June 9, 2017. https://www.christianitytoday.com/news/2017/june/southern-baptist-convention-churches-baptisms-sbc-acp.html. This news is particularly painful, and ironic, for a Christian denomination which prides itself on performing baptisms.

The Catholic Church has seen a marked decline in infant baptisms since 1965. This could be due in part to the number of infant baptisms being closely related to the number of births, which has also decreased. Even so, the number of adult baptisms has also decreased over the same time period. The number of funerals performed rose steeply from 1965-2000. From 2000 on, the number of funerals performed is now back to the 1965 level. Whether this is due to the overall number of Catholics decreasing is unclear. Center for Applied Research in the Apostolate. "Frequently Requested Church Statics." Accessed May 25, 2019. http://cara.georgetown.edu/frequently-re-quested-church-statistics/.

24   Bullard, Rev. George, Div. M. "The Life Cycle and Stages of Congregational Development." Accessed May 25, 2019. https://s3.amazonaws.com/storage.nm-storage.com/clearlakemethodist/files/stages_of_church_life_bullard.pdf

25   See my book *Green Church: Reduce, Reuse, Recycle, Rejoice!* Abingdon Press, Nashville, 2010, pages 1-11 for more on these images of God.

26   McFague, Sallie, *The Body of God: An Ecological Theology,* Fortress Press, Minneapolis, 1993, page 150.

27 Butterworth, Eric, *Spiritual Economics: The Principles and Process of True Prosperity,* Unity Books, Unity Village MO, 2001, page 17.

28 Panentheism is distinguished from pantheism, a view that says God IS everything. In *The Body of God,* page 150, Sallie McFague writes, "Panentheism is, I would suggest, a strong motif in both Hebrew and Christian traditions that take seriously the mediation of God to the world. The panentheistic tradition is found in all those passages in the Hebrew Scriptures that mediate the divine presence through human words and acts as natural phenomenon and in the New Testament in its central declaration that the 'Word was made flesh' in Jesus of Nazareth."

29 Rohr, Richard. *The Universal Christ: How a Forgotten Reality Can Change Everything We See, Hope For, and Believe,* New York: Convergent, 2019, page 239.

30 W., Bill. *Alcoholics Anonymous: The Story of How Many Thousands of Men and Women Have Recovered from Alcoholism.* New York: Alcoholics Anonymous World Services, 1976, page 85.

31 Rohr, Richard. *Radical Grace.* Cincinnati: St. Anthony Messenger Press, 1995.

32 Rohr. *Radical Grace.*

33 Oswald, Marcus. "Census Bureau: As usual, Los Alamos among nation's wealthiest counties, NM near bottom." ABQJournal.com. December 9, 2015.

https://www.abqjournal.com/688482/census-bureau-los-alamos-among-nations-wealthiest-counties-state-numbers-near-bottom.html

34 Buechner, Frederick. *Wishful Thinking: A Theological ABC.* New York: Harper & Row. 1973.

35 Straw, Julie, Mark Scullard, Susie Kukkonen, and Barry Davis, *The Work of Leaders: How Vision, Alignment, and Execution Will Change the Way You Lead,* San Francisco: John Wiley & Sons, 2013, page 5.

36 Ibid, 65.

37 Oswald, Roy M. and Arland Jacobson. *The Emotional Intelligence of Jesus: Relational Smarts for Religious Leaders,* Lanham: Rowan & Littlefield. 2015.

38 In *Creating a Culture of Renewal*®, we use the Everything DiSC® model of human behavior to develop emotional intelligence and understand congregational culture. Contact us at www.rebekahsimonpeter.com for more information.

39 MissionInsite gives detailed information, tailored for specific areas around the church, including the religious climate of the community.

40 Turow, Scott, *Ordinary Heroes,* 2005.

41 Lupton, Robert. *Toxic Charity: How Churches and Charities Hurt Those They Help (and How to Reverse It).* New York: HarperOne. 2011.

Warner, Lacey and Gaston Warner. *From Relief to Empowerment: How Your Church Can Cultivate Sustainable Mission.* The Foundry Publishing. 2017.

42 https://www.nytimes.com/interactive/2019/07/06/us/migrants-border-patrol-clint.html accessed July 7, 2019

43 Shermer, Michael, The Number of Americans with No Religious Affiliation Is Rising, April 1, 2018. https://www.scientificamerican.com/article/the-number-of-americans-with-no-religious-affiliation-is-rising/.

Other Books

from Market Square

marketsquarebooks.com

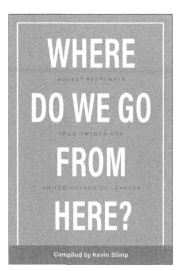

Wesleyan Grace Theology

Dr. Donald Haynes

Where Do We Go From Here?

20 United Methodist Writers

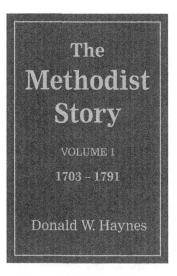

New Stories of Advent and Christmas

Charles W. Maynard

The Methodist Story
Volume I • 1703-1791

Dr. Donald Haynes

Grow Your Faith

with these books from Market Square

marketsquarebooks.com

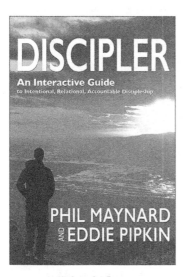

Discipler

Phil Maynard & Eddie Pipkin

Hear It, See It, Risk It

Steve Cordle

A Christian Teenager's Guide to Surviving High School

Ashley Conner

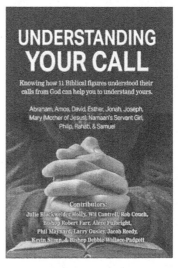

Understanding Your Call

11 Biblical Figures Understand Their Calls from God
by 10 United Methodist Leaders

Grow Your Faith

with these books from Market Square

marketsquarebooks.com

**New Stories of Advent
and Christmas**

Wil Cantrell & Paul Seay

Shift 2.0

Phil Maynard

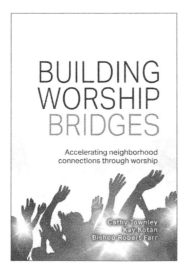

**Building Worship
Bridges**

Cathy Townley

**Get Out of
That Box!**

Anne Bosarge

Latest Titles

from Market Square Books

marketsquarebooks.com

Launching Leaders
(Leadership Development)

Kay Kotan & Phil Schroeder

From Franchise
To Local Dive

Available November 2019

The Methodist Story
Volume 2 • 1792-2019

Dr. Donald W. Haynes

Mission Possible
Revised & Expanded

Kay Kotan & Blake Bradford

Made in the USA
Monee, IL
11 July 2023

38970756R00105